# BURN
## THE
# BUSINESS
# PLAN

## Also by Carl J. Schramm

*Better Capitalism: Renewing the Entrepreneurial*
*Strength of the American Economy*
(with Robert E. Litan)

*Inside Real Innovation: How the Right Approach*
*Can Move Ideas from R&D to Market*
(with Eugene Fitzgerald and Andreas Wankerl)

*Good Capitalism, Bad Capitalism,*
*and the Economics of Growth and Prosperity*
(with William J. Baumol and Robert E. Litan)

*The Entrepreneurial Imperative:*
*How America's Economic Miracle Will*
*Reshape the World (and Change Your Life)*

*Healthcare and Its Costs*

# BURN
## THE
# BUSINESS
# PLAN

What Great Entrepreneurs Really Do

# Carl J. Schramm

JOHN
MURRAY
LEARNING

First published in United States of America in 2018 by Simon & Schuster.

This edition published in Great Britain in 2018 by John Murray Learning,
an imprint of Hodder & Stoughton. An Hachette UK company.

*British Library Cataloguing in Publication Data:* a catalogue
record for this title is available from the British Library.

Hardback: 978 1 473 67152 2
Trade Paperback: 978 1 473 60689 0
eBook: 978 1 473 60690 6

1

The publisher has used its best endeavours to ensure that any website addresses
referred to in this book are correct and active at the time of going to press.
However, the publisher and the author have no responsibility for the websites
and can make no guarantee that a site will remain live or that the
content will remain relevant, decent or appropriate.

The publisher has made every effort to mark as such all words which it
believes to be trademarks. The publisher should also like to make it clear
that the presence of a word in the book, whether marked or unmarked,
in no way affects its legal status as a trademark.

Every reasonable effort has been made by the publisher to trace the copyright
holders of material in this book. Any errors or omissions should be notified
in writing to the publisher, who will endeavour to rectify the situation for any
reprints and future editions.

Printed and bound in Great Britain by CPI Group (UK) Ltd, Croydon, CR0 4YY.

John Murray Learning policy is to use papers that are natural, renewable
and recyclable products and made from wood grown in sustainable forests.
The logging and manufacturing processes are expected to conform to
the environmental regulations of the country of origin.

Carmelite House
50 Victoria Embankment
London EC4Y 0DZ

www.hodder.co.uk

In memory of Ewing Marion Kauffman.

A great American entrepreneur who started his company without a college education, a written business plan, an incubator experience, a mentor, or a venture investor. He was committed to the idea that more people should, "Make a job, not take a job," and devoted his fortune to helping others see that entrepreneurship is a choice that anyone can make. Like so many great Americans, Ewing Kauffman saw his life's story as emblematic of how a regular person from humble beginnings could achieve success through personal initiative and hard work in a free nation that encouraged individuals to find, develop, and apply their creative talents in business. The Kauffman Foundation has embodied his magnificent choice to give back by lighting the path for those willing to take the personal risk of starting businesses that make life better for others. Thank you, Mr. K.

Carl Schramm is University Professor at Syracuse and has taught at Johns Hopkins University, MIT, and UC Davis. For ten years he was president of the Ewing Marion Kauffman Foundation, the world's leading institution supporting entrepreneurship. Schramm has founded or co-founded five companies, is an active venture investor, and has served in major corporate roles.

He was a co-founder of Global Entrepreneurship Week now celebrated in 170 countries, drafted the Startup America Act, chaired the U.S. Department of Commerce's Measuring Innovation in the Twenty-First Century Economy Advisory Committee, and was a member of the President's National Advisory Council on Innovation and Entrepreneurship. He is recognized as starting the discipline of Expeditionary Economics.

Mr Schramm lives in New York and Florida.

# Contents

# Preface

How can real, practical information help potential entrepreneurs? I have started companies, managed small and large entities, been a venture investor, consulted with big firms and governments on innovation, and spent time as a professor. For ten years, I was privileged to run the Kauffman Foundation, the "Foundation of Entrepreneurship" in Kansas City. Along the way, I was lucky enough to spend time with many successful entrepreneurs, aspiring entrepreneurs, investors, and business visionaries.

These experiences made me realize that many of the popularly held ideas about how, when, and why people start companies probably are wrong. As an economist, I began to look skeptically at the powerful underlying memes—the largely unexamined but widely accepted ideas that shape our view of the world—especially those applicable to new business success. The entrepreneurship memes seemed to be little more than an assortment of stories and case histories that had crystallized into a rubric.

So, in 2002, I embraced the opportunity to direct the Kauffman Foundation. The Foundation was a nearly $2 billion endowment established by Ewing Marion Kauffman, an innovative Kansas City pharmaceutical company founder, and was the world's largest philanthropy dedicated to promoting entrepreneurship. This was an irresistible challenge: I knew that a continuing stream of new businesses was critical to society's growth and advancement, and that what entrepreneurs really do is too important to be described by glittering narratives that are not based on evidence. After all, innovative businesses bring us unimagined products and services, create most of the new jobs in our economy, and are the most important force driving growth and creating expanding welfare. Entrepreneurs are too valuable a national resource to be subjected to a potpourri of unsubstantiated aphorisms dressed up as good business advice.

The Kauffman Foundation provided the platform to recruit a small army of brilliant economists to initiate serious research on how new businesses really get started and grow. The team extended the work of Joseph Schumpeter[1] and William Baumol,[2] two influential economists who had examined entrepreneurship well before almost anyone knew how to spell it, much less what it meant. Research inside Kauffman and scholarship supported by the Foundation produced a torrent of empirical research on entrepreneurs, which resulted in insights that people now seem to think that we've always known. For example, it was not previously well understood that young firms create more than eighty percent of all new jobs in our economy, or that new business formation plays such a significant role in economic expansion. Now, happily, entrepreneurship is embedded in every discussion about economic growth. The Kauffman team was the first to inject intellectual, empirical rigor into research about how new firms are created. Because of this work, we know much more about how businesses are formed and how they grow and what is likely to improve your chances for success.

This book seeks to translate many of these findings, and the experiences of some of the thousands of entrepreneurs whom I've met, into practical guidance and lessons. It is intended to illustrate how businesses really start, grow, and prosper. The first four chapters speak to the "what" of business startups, the following four to lessons learned by those who have gone before you, and the last section is devoted to data-derived facts, not myths, and realistic guidance from successful entrepreneurs.

# CHAPTER 1

# Burn the Business Plan

One of the headwinds that challenges a fact-based discussion of successful entrepreneurship is the looming presence of a handful of wildly successful high-tech innovators. The icons are, of course, the household names: Bill Gates, Steve Jobs, and Mark Zuckerberg, the myth-making college dropouts who became billionaires before thirty. While their stories make fascinating reading, and we owe them immeasurable gratitude for their revolutionary contributions, their narratives hold very few actionable lessons for the more than ninety-five percent of entrepreneurs who want to start a construction business, manufacture innovative building materials, become a service provider, or develop a franchise. These are the people more like you and me, from all walks of life, who want to start businesses.

In fact, the romanticized narrative of the young, mostly male, high-tech wizard accounts for the smallest constellation in the universe of entrepreneurs—only about five to seven percent. Their new businesses get almost all the high-profile investment by venture capital firms, most of the media coverage, and—here's a surprise—experience the highest failure rate of business startups. About eight in ten disappear within five years.

The real story on startups and their success rates reveals something very different. Most entrepreneurs never went to college, and most did not start their companies until they were well along in their careers. The average entrepreneur is nearly forty years old when he launches, and more than eighty percent of all new companies are started by people over thirty-five. More entrepreneurs are between forty-five and fifty-five than any other cohort, and entrepreneurs over fifty-five now create more companies than those under thirty-five. And—another surprise—the chances of a new company surviving rises with the age of the entrepreneur.

Recognizing that the "mature" entrepreneur is a significant element in the startup world also leads us to acknowledge the influence of working for someone else before you start your own company. The average entrepreneur was an employee for almost fifteen years before launching a startup. Although it may seem counterintuitive, a big company can operate as a *de facto* school in which you can learn how to—and sometimes how *not* to—test, manufacture, price, and sell products; organize a workforce and deal with suppliers; finance equipment and facilities; and comply with legal and regulatory requirements. Research also tells us that a significant number of innovative entrepreneurs have launched out of large companies that didn't want to diversify to invest in what they saw as a tangent to their core businesses. Some established companies even have signed over ownership of innovative ideas to employees and sent them off with good wishes for success.

## Planning, then Pivoting,
## then Pivoting, then Pivoting

Early in the history of the Internet, a raft of businesses started within months of one another, all premised on the thesis that commerce was moving to what was then known as the "World Wide Web." Most of these startups were described in Silicon Valley shorthand as "B2C," business to consumer, companies. Amazon, founded in July 1994, was one. Another group of companies, "B2B," emerged to conduct bigger transactions between companies. Michael Levin was ready to play.

Levin went to the University of Wisconsin to study international relations before going to Harvard for an MBA. After graduating, he went to work for an international steel trading firm, and eventually acquired the company. Among other activities, Levin's business involved buying the future production of steel mills in, say, China, with a plan to sell it a few months later at a higher price to factories making steel products in other countries.

As the frenzy of Internet commerce grew—now remembered as the dot-com era—Levin developed the idea of an online market for steel. After talking with customers about the feasibility of trading on the Internet, he came to believe that he might have a good idea for a B2B business. Next, he went to Silicon Valley to sell his story. Given his industry experience, past success, and readiness to invest some of his own money, venture firms were enthusiastic. They backed him on the spot, even though he presented only a few slides.

While he was organizing his new company, Levin's investors asked him to develop a detailed business plan complete with sales forecasts and budgets. Once underway, ensconced in nice offices with a team of programmers and a state-of-the-art website, Levin's startup came face-to-face with reality. Steelmakers who sold, and factory customers who bought, didn't want to abandon the old ways of trading steel. They liked the face-to-face bargaining over multimillion dollar contracts, and the steak dinners and golf outings that were part of the tradition. Sales on his Internet-based trading platform were not materializing.

While the B2B steel-trading business was failing, unexpectedly, both steelmakers and steel users were expressing strong interest in using the portion of the new company's computer models that forecast prices. In addition, they wanted to buy access to the company's customized supply-chain software. Levin's board was unimpressed. The vision that he had laid down in his plan had convinced his investors that the steel market eventually would see the virtues of B2B trading. Levin had written a plan that was too convincing. He found it impossible to persuade his board that the company should pivot to become a software supplier. Levin eventually bought out his investors and his startup became a software business, one of the few B2B startups that still survives.

B2C businesses, on the other hand, flourished. New ones open every day selling everything imaginable, as well as renting out everything from used dresses and fur coats to spare bedrooms.

Levin returned to his old business, trading steel, one contract at a time, on the phone, or in face-to-face meetings, with useful acquired wisdom. "Business plans are like a religious ritual. If you write one, success is supposed to follow. In the case of my startup, the investors really believed in the plan, and any adjustments responding to real customer demand, like selling software, was read as a dangerous step that put in jeopardy the future envisioned in the plan." In Levin's words, "Making a successful company requires an intimate tango with customers, not a tight grip on a business plan."

My own entrepreneurial journey began when I was a junior professor at Johns Hopkins in Baltimore. Healthcare economics was my field, and one of my particular areas of interest was whether hospital "monopolies"—which was, at the time, the way that the Federal Trade Commission defined ownership by a hospital company of more than one hospital in the same market—resulted in price fixing. Obviously, by the FTC's use of the pejorative "monopoly," they believed that the answer to that question was "yes," and they posited that such price fixing meant higher hospital prices for patients and their insurers in a "monopoly" market. On the other hand, hospital companies asserted that owning more than one hospital in the same market achieved cost efficiencies that saved money for patients and insurance companies.

My research as an academic economist focused on quantitative healthcare issues, and I was asked both by hospital companies and the federal government to research this issue and report on my findings. The project required assembling more accounting and clinical data on hospitals than had ever before been brought together. I gathered billing records for every hospital in four states, as well as anonymous data on hundreds of thousands of their patients. This was a "big data" project before the term was even in use.[1] While analyzing the statistics, I came across an unexpected and what seemed to me to be a rather astonishing fact: even standardizing for income levels, patients at some lower-cost hospitals had better healthcare outcomes than patients at higher-cost hospitals, which seemed to indicate that they were receiving better care.

With a lot more research and number crunching, the data showed that hospitals could cut costs and, at the same time, improve the quality of care. Best of all, the numbers that I'd collected clearly demonstrated how those hospitals could operate more effectively, and I was able to explain it.

This discovery upset my career plan. I could write another academic paper to explain my findings—knowing, though, that no matter how widely it might be read in scholarly or even industry circles, hospitals would not take it upon themselves to design and implement the actual mechanics and systems to improve their patient care and lower their prices.

As I saw it, my only other option was to develop, sell, and install decision-support systems so that hospitals could achieve the win-win outcomes that were possible. This posed a difficult dilemma. Hopkins frowned on faculty members becoming involved in businesses. I'd have to resign my professorship. I felt like the lone traveler in Robert Frost's poem "The Road Not Taken"; not only would I be leaving a great university, but I'd be stepping away from a steady, if not exactly copious, financial sinecure. If I took the leap, I'd have to look to my fragile little startup not only to fund itself but to pay my salary as well. To make the decision even more difficult, just as this quandary began to unfold, my wife and I had bought a new house and become first-time parents. For the next few years, I would have very few good nights' sleep and always thanked my lucky stars that my wife was employed and could put beans on the table if everything went to hell.

In the early years, most startups face particular financial stress. When my little company's revenues looked like they would be insufficient to acquire data, buy computers, and hire needed staff—mostly former Hopkins students—my banker advised me to talk with one of the newly formed venture capital funds in the area. The ensuing meeting was a scene out of a movie. After hearing my story, the investor put his feet up on his desk, lit a cigar, and lectured me about how professors made bad businessmen. Presuming all investors would say the same thing, we tightened our belts. We spent no more than our revenue. I later learned that this approach to self-funding was known as "bootstrapping."

Like many first-time entrepreneurs, I had no relevant experience. I had to feel my way along every day. No one, including my bank, ever suggested writing a business plan. If they had, it surely wouldn't have helped.

Also like many first-time entrepreneurs, I was sure that my product was so revolutionary that customers would rush to buy it. But, much to my consternation, sales did not come easily and the price that the market was willing to pay didn't come close to what I thought that my product was worth or even what it would cost to produce. I learned that hospitals didn't much care about efficiency and, frankly, they didn't seem to care that much about the better patient outcomes that might result. At that time, hospitals were being paid on a cost-plus basis by the federal government and insurance companies so, to them, efficiency was an interesting public policy discussion but hardly worth upsetting doctors, nurses, and administrators. Even worse, when talking with some hospitals' lawyers, I learned that they were very uncomfortable having data on patient outcomes in their possession, which could prove embarrassing and perhaps result in liability if made public. Essentially, hospitals and their lawyers were afraid to focus on improving the quality of care because that would imply that the quality of care could be improved. My product, which could have saved hospitals lots of money and produced better care in the bargain, faced indifference and even active resistance from those who ran the enterprises and sought to protect their institutions.

My reflex was to "blame the customer" for being too dumb to know what was good for them. I realized, much more slowly than I should have, that I couldn't convince hospitals to buy my better mousetrap. I had to find a different customer. Fortunately, in the company's second year, it finally dawned on me that all hospital construction was financed with debt. New buildings were funded by long-maturity bonds that repaid investors' capital in thirty years but also paid interest yearly from the hospital's current income.

Just like the first cousin of hospital bonds, the municipal bond, hospital debt had to be insured to protect investors in the event of a hospital's bankruptcy. If the companies selling hospital bond insurance could know that Hospital A was run more efficiently than Hospital B, they could better estimate their comparative risk and set premiums accordingly.

When I appeared for my first sales call to a company that sold hospital bond insurance, the chief underwriter nearly kissed me. "I knew you'd show up one day!" he said. Of course, he didn't mean me, personally. Rather, he knew that there had to be a quantitative way to judge the financial strength of hospitals as well as to forecast whether a given institution might be more at risk for unfavorable patient outcomes, which in his world meant the increased risk of high-dollar malpractice verdicts.

Within a few years, the company that my students and I had created for one type of customer was sold to another type of customer, an insurer, and I found myself a part of an industry that I didn't know existed when I left the university to launch a business.

## Dancing, Not Planning

Anyone who has started a business can appreciate these stories. Businesses never evolve according to the pre-set plan. Just as in war, of which Von Moltke said, "No plan survives first contact with the enemy," it is rare to find an entrepreneur who reports that his business plan was of much use. Business is simply too fluid; unpredictable markets set the direction of companies for established giants and small startups alike, not the other way around. Entrepreneurs must learn to dance to the market's ever-changing tempo and rhythm. Planning doesn't help and is mostly a waste of time.

Nevertheless, anyone thinking about starting a business will encounter one universal piece of advice—write a business plan.

If a would-be entrepreneur wants to get a Small Business Administration (SBA) loan, the government requires a written business plan, one that conforms to the specific model explored below. Similarly, banks now are required by federal regulators to have business plans on file for any new companies to which they lend money. It is impossible for someone without connections to get a meeting with a venture capital firm without a written plan. Every angel investor and mentor will insist on a written plan from anyone wanting their attention. Within a remarkably short period—fewer than thirty years—business plan writing has emerged as the entrepreneur's Rosetta Stone. It is, as Levin says, "something of a religious ritual."

So powerful is the idea that business planning will lead to a successful startup that at least three million plans are written every year. Why? Tens of millions of people dream of emulating the entrepreneurs of Silicon Valley. Kauffman Foundation studies show that over half of all adults, and more than seventy percent of all college students, want to become entrepreneurs.

It is hard not to be fascinated by people who turn an idea into a company and become wealthy within a few years. Every year there are movies about entrepreneurs; there are four feature-length films about Steve Jobs alone. Monthly magazines, including *Entrepreneur*, *Inc.*, *Wired*, and *Fast Company*, tell the stories of startups like the Dollar Shave Club, created in 2011 to sell better razors on the Internet, that are bought by giant companies, in that case Unilever, four years later for $1 billion. *Shark Tank*, a popular cable show, glamorizes investors who want to make money by betting on the business plans of entrepreneurs. Successful entrepreneurs are larger-than-life figures, hobnobbing with movie stars and politicians. It is no wonder that Syracuse Professor Robert Thompson, who studies pop culture, says that creating a startup "is taking up a larger and larger role in our aspirational lives."

## Everyman and the Princes

This book is for those who think that they might want to start a business someday. It is for *Everyman*, a medieval term describing regular people. Most people who start companies are like you: They've never come close to meeting a venture-capital investor; never studied entrepreneurship in college; have never heard of a business incubator; and never wrote a business plan.

Ninety-five percent of Everyman entrepreneurs are very different from the "rock star" princes of Silicon Valley. The princes rightly are regarded as geniuses, not only for giving us wondrous new technology, but also for their abilities to grow their ideas into enormous businesses. Perhaps even more important, but as a side effect, they have rekindled America's interest in how businesses are born.

Most of the companies started by these princes can trace their roots back to the discovery of the semiconductor in 1947. This extraordinary device allowed solid-state electronics to emerge, which, twenty years later, enabled the computer and accompanying software revolutions. By an accident of fate—or maybe the beautiful weather?—the semiconductor revolution started in Northern California's Silicon Valley. It was there that some of America's most extraordinary firms were created in the late 1960s and the following decades, including Adobe, Apple, Cisco, Fairchild Semiconductor, Intel, Intuit, Oracle, and Sun Microsystems. (Bill Gates and Paul Allen started Microsoft in Albuquerque.)

For most of the previous century, opening a new store or starting a manufacturing company wasn't much remarked upon. Starting a business wasn't very noteworthy, mostly because there were many more individual stand-alone businesses, and many more being started. For example, nearly half the veterans returning from World

War II eventually started companies. "Business owners"—not then known as entrepreneurs—were more common; your neighbor was much more likely to work for himself than he is today.

When I was in high school in the 1960s, America's business heroes were men like Alexander Graham Bell who had invented many of the things that we use every day. Also among these heroes were Willis Carrier, George Eastman, Thomas Edison, and the Wright brothers, who gave us, respectively, air conditioning, cameras, light bulbs, and airplanes. They were the inventor saints—inspirational and dead—and were studied and remembered more for what they had invented, not for the companies that they had started: AT&T, Carrier, Kodak, General Electric, and Curtiss-Wright (which once made many of the world's airplanes).

The great inventors started companies before there was a professional cadre of advisers to new businesses. Indeed, as recently as 1980, there were fewer than ten professors in all of the nation's business schools who paid any attention to how new businesses began. The subject never seemed of much interest to academics. Back then, no one went to college to learn how to start a business, nor was there any particular interest in how that happened. Then, nearly all students in business schools planned, upon graduation, to take a job in an established giant corporation, hoping to climb the corporate ladder to an executive position.

This all changed during the 1980s when business students became interested in emulating Gates and Jobs. Seeing their students ready to forego careers as managers in big companies to start their own companies, business professors responded with courses like "New Venture Creation" and "Cases in New Business," names that today sound clunky and naive. There were no courses on "entrepreneurship." The word "entrepreneur" was not even in common use until well into the 1980s.

## Birth of the Business Plan

Today, a small army of academics, about six thousand professors and instructors, teach entrepreneurship. Nearly all their courses embrace what has become a convention, a two-part doctrine believed critical to producing successful new businesses. The first is that every new company should start with a written description of the firm, designed to appeal to venture investors. Second is the belief that the chance of success for any new business is improved if it incubates in a supportive entrepreneurial ecosystem.

Understanding how these two touchstones evolved is important to illuminating a critically important contradiction: The more widely these precepts are followed, the fewer new companies result.

Business plan writing was invented in response to the explosion of entrepreneurial activity in the 1980s. The idea of planning was borrowed from the study of business strategy, which historically was one of the original and core disciplines of business school training. Strategic planning traditionally focused on guiding giant corporations through complex decisions such as whether to build a new plant, globalize the supply chain, or acquire another firm. The methodology involved detailed analysis of such ideas and their implications for the company's finances and its long-term well-being. Historically, strategic planning tools were not applied to the process of starting a business from scratch, and for good reason.

None of America's great companies, those for which business professors were preparing the next generation of managers in bygone days, had started with written plans. Nearly all of *Fortune* magazine's legacy 100 companies, including American Airlines, Disney, DuPont, General Electric, General Motors, Exxon (begun as Standard Oil), Ford, IBM, Johnson & Johnson, Procter & Gamble, McKesson, and Xerox, started without plans. If any of those founders did any writing, it was likely on the back of envelopes or, as was the genesis of Southwest Airlines, on a napkin. Southwest's route map, including cities to which it plans to fly in the future, continues to appear on its in-flight cocktail napkins, paying homage to the map first drawn by Herb Kelleher, the line's founder.

As we will see again and again, the methodology imported from strategic planning makes no sense in the context of entrepreneurial startups. Nonetheless, with little else to draw upon, early instructors restyled the corporate-planning template, identifying the eleven elements that they believed should be known and described before starting a new company.[2]

This approach to planning suggests that entrepreneurs can achieve success by pursuing a linear, rational, critical path model, one completely unrelated to the spontaneous trial-and-error process that characterizes the inevitably messy early years of every startup. Planning is nothing more than an attempt to bring order to a process that is chaotic by nature, and plan writing a technique that provides structure to the academic exercise.

In promoting the planning model, the first generation of entrepreuneurship instructors overlooked another salient reality. None of the newly forming high-tech startups, which were the spark that had ignited the demand for courses on how to start a business—and many of which had ascended to the *Fortune 100* list—had begun with written business plans. Wozniak and Jobs never wrote a plan for Apple. Like their predecessors a century before, the founders of Cisco, Hewlett-Packard, Google, Nike, Oracle, and Walmart started companies without plans. Today, Microsoft sells software to support business-plan writing, but Bill Gates and Paul Allen never wrote one to start Microsoft. Intel's plan, preserved at the company's museum, famously barely fills one poorly typewritten page. It's really a mission statement that has no forecasts, discussions about competing products, descriptors of barriers to entry, and not a word about how the company will make money, each important parts of the prevailing business planning model.

Four decades after business planning became the established centerpiece of the textbook entrepreneurial experience, many of today's fastest-growing startups, including Facebook, Gilt Groupe, and Twitter, began without written plans.

## Plans Are for Investors

One reason that the formalized business plan took root so quickly, apart from the fact that there was no other instructional format on offer, was that venture investors embraced the idea with a vengeance. Venture investing was itself invented in the early 1970s to help many of the exciting computer and software firms in Silicon Valley get started. Formed as new financial entities known as venture capital funds, VCs provided capital for technology startups that commercial banks and conventional lenders couldn't understand and considered too risky. These new funds, which were banklike businesses themselves, were willing to embrace more risk because the money that they were investing came from investors, including university and foundation endowments, that were willing to withstand short-term losses in anticipation of larger returns in the future. These were uncertainties that the investment guidelines of pension funds and life insurance companies, the other major sources of capital, couldn't tolerate.

Early venture investments in companies like Intel and Apple paid out enormous multiples on the initially invested capital when those companies sold shares to the public. So extraordinary were these early returns, often achieving thirty percent annually on invested capital, that dozens of new venture funds crowded into Silicon Valley. This was a natural symbiosis; more entrepreneurs starting more new firms produced more opportunities for more investors. And, the employees of many startups often moved on to start their own companies.

As the number of venture funds grew, the business plan became a kind of handy model, much like the Common App, a form now used by high-school students that allows them to simultaneously apply to multiple colleges. The uniform business plan made the job of comparing proposed startup ideas much easier for investors; it became a kind of shorthand. Of course, the primary interest of venture investors, who by definition had short-term returns in mind, was the plan's description of how soon the company could get to a "liquidity event," that is, the moment at which another company would buy the startup or the startup would sell shares to the public in an "initial public offering" (IPO). Being acquired, or "going public," was the last step, the "exit strategy" required in every business plan.

Business planning, with its emphasis on the exit, has changed the very nature of what many people see as the reason for creating new businesses in the first place. Every plan now begins with a description of the new idea that it will bring to the market. The necessary intermediate steps are geared toward getting the startup ready for the exit. The use of formal plans has changed the essential purpose of many startups, a motivation that is new to the age-old process of starting companies. Now, in many cases, the formal plan transforms the startup into a vehicle for getting to an ASAP payday for entrepreneurs and investors. One author argues that, "'Built to flip' should not be a dirty phrase or unnatural act. I believe that to succeed today, entrepreneurs must not only aspire to early exits, but design that objective into their corporate structures and corporate DNA"—and argues that, from start to finish, a new business should occupy its founder for no more than four years.[3]

Not one of the entrepreneurs who started *Fortune 100* firms ever treated their companies like house flippers, inventing a business in order to get out with a profit as quickly as possible. Great companies in the past were not created to be transactional properties; they were built to last for decades to come. The credo of Johnson & Johnson, carved on a stone plinth in the lobby of the company's headquarters, tells of J&J's purpose to indefinitely serve the needs of its customers, provide good jobs to its employees, and earn a fair return for its shareholders.[4]

## It Takes a Village

Inspired by a mistaken reading of the garage-band-all-nighter litany that made Silicon Valley the cradle of so many high-tech companies, academic experts began to argue that, in addition to the value of writing formal business plans, entrepreneurs would be more likely to succeed if they were supported by a local "ecosystem." This idea was embraced by community leaders, particularly in urban areas that were experiencing manufacturing decline and flight, as a means of revitalizing local economies. As a result, every major city now boasts an integrated set of resources, assembled in *incubators*, created to support and encourage local entrepreneurs. This "ecosystem" formula requires a locally focused, often publicly financed and professionally managed venture fund; organized groups of amateur or angel investors; a network of business people who have experience starting companies and are ready to serve as mentors; and physical spaces where new firms can locate—often at low or no rent—to be "incubated" during their development.

In addition to these resources, many communities have restored or rebuilt entire neighborhoods designed to be congenial to the "creative class," loosely defined as young urban dwellers thought to include entrepreneurs.[5] To visit some of these districts is to believe that entrepreneurs must live in lofts and be surrounded by art galleries and craft breweries. So widespread is the vision that entrepreneurship and hip neighborhoods go together that we see universities teaching students of urban planning and architecture to study the lifestyles of small groups of "urban entrepreneurs," including leather-goods artisans and herbal compounders, in order to envision a physical environment that will produce more of them.

Taken together, the two touchstones of entrepreneurial success—writing a business plan and finding your way into a startup ecosystem for support and inspiration—form the prevailing narrative of today's so-called startup process. A small industry exists that is dedicated to advancing this narrative to increase the number of new firms and enhance the probability of their success. The federal government provides at least $2 billion annually—the exact number being too murky to actually quantify beyond that likely low estimate—to support these efforts, including grants to universities to teach entrepreneurship and to support local ecosystems.

Unfortunately, however, there is now solid, quantitative evidence to suggest that this prevailing narrative, and the activities of institutions receiving substantial amounts of federal, state, and local funds, doesn't work.

In fact, following the narrative's prescriptions seems to produce the opposite of the intended result: As more business plans are written, and as more local ecosystems are created, the number of startup businesses continues to fall.

Data reaching back to 1980 shows that about 700,000 new firms were started every year in the United States. That number began to decline just as the prevailing narrative, which was developed explicitly to *increase* the number of entrepreneurs and to improve their chances of success, took hold. The evidence shows an indisputable inverse relationship. As more professors teach new-business planning, as more venture capital is available, and as more local ecosystems, revolving around incubators, came to exist, the number of new firms has steadily declined.

In 2016, fewer than 500,000 new companies were born.

In addition, new business failure rates remain unchanged since 1992, the first year for which there are reliable data. Today, just as in 1992, one-quarter of startups do not survive their first year; more than half are out of business at five years; and fewer than twenty percent exist in ten. The boomerang effect of targeting more resources to attempt to encourage and support more entrepreneurs, yet seeing fewer and fewer businesses start, leads to the unavoidable conclusion that what we are doing is not merely misguided but likely harmful.

## What Went Wrong?

In retrospect it is not surprising that the first professors of entrepreneurship—who saw writing business plans and creating entrepreneurial ecosystems as necessary to improve the success of startups—were mistaken. The first attempts to explain complex social phenomena in almost any new field often get off on the wrong foot.

In the 1930s, for example, many economists, then members of a young discipline, explained the Great Depression using a biological metaphor. They said that the economy had matured and we would never again see rapid growth. How could they have known any better? There were no historic statistics measuring growth, employment, income, or prices. Today's empirical economic analysis, depending on computers full of time-series data and elaborate forecasting models, was decades in the future.

When market demand came upon the academy from students wanting to learn how exciting new companies were started, instructors had little information upon which to draw to unravel those mysteries. There remain only a handful of case studies of the early years of many big businesses. Even in today's data-driven world, the federal government has no accurate count of the number of new businesses created every year. It was not until 2006, that the Kauffman Foundation established the first ongoing survey of new firms that, over time, will enable us to develop fact-based approaches to supporting and encouraging the new firms of the future.

Even absent data in the 1980s, however, the default to a planning model to guide aspiring entrepreneurs wasn't exactly logical, as the planning process was already being questioned. In the late 1970s, Israeli scientists Daniel Kahneman and Amos Tversky identified what they called the "planning fallacy."[6] Simply put, their research concluded that optimism is endemic to humans when they plan. Kahneman won the Nobel Prize in 2002, in part because of his insight into what is now called "behavioral economics," which confirmed how feeble rational planning models are when subjected to the vagaries of market behavior.

Robert Bruner's analysis of decades of corporate mergers—those transactions that are the subject of the most sophisticated business planning imaginable—confirmed the findings of Harvard economist Albert Hirschman that roughly eighty percent of implemented plans did not meet their objectives.[7] Bruner showed that eighty percent of acquisitions, usually of smaller firms by bigger ones, failed to meet their anticipated contributions to the larger firm's earnings. This same analysis of the actual efficacy of high-quality analysis and business planning pertains in other related venues.

For example, my own analysis of a sample of university business-plan contest winners presents an even worse record. During the five years studied, fewer than one in eight of the prize-winning businesses were started and, of those, fewer than ten percent survived even three years.

Entrepreneurial ecosystems have proven no more helpful than plan writing in increasing the number of new firms. Despite over two hundred cities having established districts expressly designated as "entrepreneur friendly," there is no conclusive evidence that local ecosystems produce any more entrepreneurs than if they had never been established or existed. A confirming indicator is that only one of the 236 local publicly supported venture funds established over the last twenty years has produced a positive return to its taxpayer investors.

Despite any evidence of its success, the prevailing two-part narrative of writing a plan continues to focus on winning the financial support of venture capitalists, and leveraging local ecosystems. But, paradoxically, faced with a system that fails eighty percent of those who try it, there appears to be no entrepreneurial impulse to make starting a firm a better, faster, or a more certain process.

## Are You an Entrepreneur?

In fact, the four most important questions for entrepreneurs are not answered in entrepreneurship courses.

The first is whether you *are* an entrepreneur. Asking this question of a professor of entrepreneurship, a professional investor, or a successful entrepreneur is likely to trigger a fruitless discussion about whether entrepreneurs are "born" or "made," that is, whether an entrepreneur is birthed with special talents or if she, somewhere along the way, was in an environment that nurtured the skills needed to create a successful business. Some experts throw in the unhelpful view that entrepreneurs are people who are more comfortable with risk, while others pronounce with equal certainty that entrepreneurs are more cautious and deliberate personalities.

So, how can you determine if you really are an entrepreneur? The first step is to appreciate who entrepreneurs are by understanding just what it is that they do:

**An entrepreneur is someone who exploits an innovative idea—one that he develops, or copies, improves, or rents—to start a profit-seeking, scalable business that successfully satisfies demand for a new or better product.**

Because the identity of an entrepreneur is defined by action, not intent or aspiration, this definition is meaningful only through experience. No one who has not started a business can really know what it is to be an entrepreneur. Studying the three elements of this definition can help you to understand if you really want to do the things that entrepreneurs do.

A new business must first have a product or service that is sufficiently novel, or that the market will perceive to be better than that which exists, so that demand will materialize. If you are an *innovator–entrepreneur*, you will create the idea for your new company. Most of today's entrepreneurs, however, do not themselves generate the ideas for their businesses. Rather, they see that there is a market need and offer improved products, services, or business processes that are better than what already exists. Or, they rent or buy access to another's innovative idea.

Second, entrepreneurs create profit-seeking companies.[8] They start businesses intent on making money now and expecting that the equity value of their firms will continually increase in the future. Profit-making startups are critical to our economy; new companies are the source of most of our economic growth. As new firms start and grow, those less than five years old create about eighty percent of all new jobs. Those jobs, in turn, contribute to the economy's ability to create more innovation and wealth in the future. Also, as you will see, innovation can beget innovation; many of our most innovative and fastest-growing companies spawn additional startups.

The pursuit of growth is the third defining characteristic of entrepreneurial firms. Expansion of any organization, other than government, is a sure sign of its economic value and health. Every entrepreneur wants to "scale" her company to make it bigger, better, faster, and more profitable.

This book is unlikely to be helpful to the person whose happy life's work is to own a single hair salon, be a freelance photographer, or work as an artisan glass blower making one-of-a-kind objects. Our society is immeasurably enriched by the talents and satisfaction that such people derive from their work and the products and services that they provide to their customers, but they should not be confused with entrepreneurs. Contrast the person who starts a store to supply artists and craftspeople, with no ambition to open a second location, with Michael Dupey, who started Michael's Arts and Crafts in 1976 and now operates 1,200 stores nationwide. Entrepreneurs, by nature, want to build and grow companies.

## What Kind of Entrepreneur Are You?

The second question you must confront is what kind of entrepreneur you will choose to be. As we well know, today's prevailing narrative is shaped largely by high-tech startups in which every entrepreneur was first seen as an innovating genius. Innovator–entrepreneurs create new businesses based on technologies that they invented.

But every other type of entrepreneur experiences more success. About fifteen percent of all startups are created by company employees who find themselves in a spin-out situation, where an existing company chooses to dispose of a line of business that it has determined is no longer within their core mission or perhaps is not worthy of the additional investment needed to achieve real success and scale. Other employees, who become frustrated by their employer's lack of support for an idea, product, or service that the employee believes could improve the company's future, strike out on their own to turn that spurned idea into a new venture. And others, sometimes called *discovery entrepreneurs*, typically university scientists, start great companies using the new ideas that grew out of their years of research. The five-year success rates for spin-out and discovery entrepreneurs is about forty percent.

Eighty percent of entrepreneurs are "replicative," a term coined by Professor William Baumol to describe people who copy, and usually improve, existing and successful ideas with the intent to own a successful and growing business.[9] These entrepreneurs do not build businesses motivated by the need to get their innovative idea to market in the form of a new product. Half of this group—about forty percent of all startups—are created as franchises, that is, new businesses in which an entrepreneur buys or rents the business idea from another entrepreneur whose innovative idea requires a network of other entrepreneurs to reach scale. Owners of strong franchises like Holiday Inns, Jimmy John's, or Dunkin' Donuts experience the lowest rates of failure of any enterprises, with more than ninety percent surviving ten years. Five-year survival rates across all franchises, both brand-new and well-established, average about thirty percent.

The remaining forty percent of startups, also replicative by nature, are unaffiliated retail businesses that sell everything from auto repairs to zippers. The merchant–entrepreneurs who start these enterprises see a market for something new, or a better way to promote and sell already existing goods.

Jack O'Neill, an early surfing enthusiast from Santa Cruz, California, began experimenting with neoprene to make a warm, waterproof jacket, so that he could surf in colder parts of the ocean. Eventually he glued together the first wetsuit, and opened a store to sell them.

John Mackey, working in a food co-op in 1980, came up with a way to market organic food beyond the demographic of counter-culture aging hippies, and determined that he could build a business by targeting younger shoppers with a growing interest in how their food was sourced. Whole Foods really began as just a grocery store selling in a different way—and now, after its acquisition by Amazon, yet a new different way will begin.

The prevailing entrepreneurial narrative, formed around high-tech innovators, gives little attention to people starting "stores." One reason is that single stores, including neighborhood restaurants, gyms, and clothing boutiques, experience failure rates second only to Silicon Valley–type innovator–entrepreneurs, with fewer than thirty percent surviving five years. But merchants, including Jeff Bezos, who created Amazon, and Bernie Marcus, whose Home Depot changed the way that hardware, tools, paint, lumber, and shrubs and trees for your yard are sold, created stores that are much more. They play an important role in making retailing work better for customers and, importantly, for product and service entrepreneurs who use those stores as channels to reach enormous markets.

Bezos and Marcus illustrate another aspect of entrepreneurial success. Whichever kind of entrepreneur you may start out to be, including franchisees who buy fully developed business models and merchants whose first idea is just to open a single store, the chances are that you will become an innovator along the way. It is the very nature of business to solve problems in creative ways. Every entrepreneur seeks to make his product better, faster, and cheaper, to turn his store into a setting that will attract more customers, operate more efficiently, increase his profit, and build a more successful company.

## How Can You Succeed?

Given the odds that four out of five startups fail in their first ten years, the most important question for anyone thinking about becoming an entrepreneur is how to avoid failure. Successful entrepreneurs seem to share three characteristics. Do they describe you?

First, appearances notwithstanding—and often notwithstanding the revised hindsight recollections of successful entrepreneurs themselves—most entrepreneurs prepare for a long time before actually starting a company. While many entrepreneurs look back on their decisions to start a company in prose that suggests a thunderclap or a Biblical revelation, most had an intuition that they might become entrepreneurs well before they actually acted. Many budding entrepreneurs are like corporate CEOs who, twenty years before they achieve the corner office, recall almost unconsciously preparing themselves for the C-suite. Long before their ambitions were apparent, in some cases even to themselves, they attentively watched the corporate decision making process, projecting themselves hypothetically into their bosses' shoes and asking themselves what they would do in the circumstances.

Richard Branson tells of becoming an entrepreneur by a happy "mistake," calling his first record company "Virgin" because, he said, he knew nothing about business. In fact, Branson had worked in the record business in his high school days. Along the way, by observing how the industry worked, he formed views about better ways to make records, pay artists, and market music. In short, long before starting his company, Branson had developed a comprehensive critique of the industry that he was about to revolutionize. He had a very clear idea of how he would take a very different approach to running a record company.

A second characteristic of success involves a certain kind of mental flexibility, being able to change direction as circumstances require while keeping a clear line of sight to the goal of building a successful company. Michael Levin saw opportunity even when his investors would not change their vision of where success was to be found for his startup. The rigidity of a business plan is antithetical to a good entrepreneur's inclination to respond to opportunity and to shifting facts and circumstances.

A new business, no matter how carefully planned, always proves to be a platform for unexpected innovation. When Henry Ford was frustrated that he could not make his cars affordable when building them one at a time, as he had done in his first two companies—both of which failed—he borrowed the idea of the assembly line from the meatpacking industry. Ford flourished while hundreds of competitors, committed to conventional production methods, failed.

Aspiring to build a big company is the third characteristic of successful entrepreneurs. Daniel Burnham, the city planner responsible for Chicago's beautiful waterfront, which he designed more than a century ago, famously said, "Make no little plans; they have no magic to stir men's blood."

Every entrepreneur faces a decision that is fundamentally economic. Can you maximize your income and your ability to accumulate wealth by starting a business? Because the failure rate of new businesses is so high, even in enterprises with the best rates of success, every potential entrepreneur must consider that a decision to start a business may mean that he or she will experience lower overall lifetime earnings and may end up building fewer personal assets than those who elect to remain employees for their working lives. This is a hard and risk-laden reality to confront.

With this in mind, every aspiring entrepreneur should think

twice about starting a new business if the business he dreams of cannot grow to scale or if she is not really committed to managing and growing a company.

The bigger a business gets, the more likely that it will survive and then thrive. Risk decreases as businesses become larger because larger enterprises accumulate resources, using them to support continuing innovation as well as beat or buy new competitors.

Size also allows for more efficiency, which, in business, always leads to expanding profit. Sam Walton, for example, transformed the lives of millions of people when he started Walmart. He was inspired to start a store as a means to get better goods to poor people, particularly those in rural areas, whom he believed were paying too much for inferior products. Walton's great innovation was managing his company's supply chain, a term that he helped to champion, by controlling products from the manufacturer's factory to his shelves. He had to grow to massive size to capture the efficiencies needed for Walmart to provide better clothes, televisions, and groceries at lower prices—a pricing revolution that, we now know, has resulted in Walmart's competitors offering lower prices across a range of consumer items, and overall savings to American shoppers, whether they shop at Walmart or not, of at least $630 per household per year.[10]

## Will You Have an Entrepreneurial Moment?

In the pages ahead you will meet many entrepreneurs. None of them live in Silicon Valley. A few have a touch of genius. Most, however, are regular people with educations and job experiences much like your own. Only one started a company while under thirty, when entrepreneurial failures are most common. Five wrote plans; one described a business that worked: he wrote it only when his product had already been tested and ready, and when he needed money.

Each of these individuals has, or had, unique reasons for deciding to take a step that most would have seen as fraught with risk, but a path that each knew could change the course of their lives. These entrepreneurial moments happened when the budding entrepreneurs assessed that the potential returns of devoting their lives to starting a company seemed greater than the perceived dangers involved. Not one of these entrepreneurs foresaw creating the companies they launched as their career goals. Rather, it seemed to be a natural next step.

The real magic in the stories ahead has to do with why anyone would want to become an entrepreneur. It is why you are reading this book. If you are successful, you might become rich and maybe even famous. More important, however, you may be happier. Nearly a century ago, Abraham Maslow, a psychologist who studied happiness, concluded that, when someone is able to invent new solutions to human needs and to see their solutions valued in the marketplace, they achieve a kind of happiness that he called "self-actualization." Successful entrepreneurs come to believe that the best use of their experience, skills, and education is the building of new businesses. They seem to see their talents used in ways that are more authentic, resonating with a higher purpose in life.

A 2013 global survey reported that successful entrepreneurs are among the happiest people on earth. Making money by improving, or even just making more enjoyable, the lives of millions of others with something that you created is the reason that entrepreneurs tackle the unknowns and risks that they do. If your destiny is to become an entrepreneur, you should know how to achieve success, which involves avoiding failure. Ahead, you'll meet people who figured this out and who are sure that their chosen path has made them, and others, happier.

---

# CHAPTER 2

# Twelve Things Every Aspiring Entrepreneur Should Know

At one point in my career, I was recruited to be the CEO of a health insurance company, a subsidiary of an international behemoth. It was the most frustrating job of my life. I saw the health insurance industry as one that could be transformed by new techniques to analyze data, push ahead on innovative coverage and claims processes to provide better and less complex service to customers, and get a better handle on how insurers paid hospitals and doctors.

Instead, I learned firsthand that success often is the enemy of innovation. The holding company chairman repeatedly told me, "Don't mess with the formula. You are running our most profitable company. Just keep paying the claims."

I eventually quit and started a firm through which I could invest in promising startups in health informatics and risk management. Soon, I also was scouting for new, innovative startups for major companies as well as venture funds in Silicon Valley. Perhaps because I was trained as a researcher, I was curious about whether there were any obvious traits or characteristics of new startups and their founder-entrepreneurs that could predict success or failure. Venture investors spoke with certainty about being able to discern a great idea by reading business plans and talking to entrepreneurs, but when I asked about the criteria that they used to judge the good from the bad, they offered formulaic answers. A common one was, "Is the company's product like aspirin?" That is, does it solve an existing problem? Or does the entrepreneur have to invent the problem, too?

When I became a limited partner in a famous venture fund, I was puzzled to learn that, after years of experience, they were still stuck at achieving only one real hit for about every ten companies they'd backed. Five or six of every ten picks failed quickly and a few limped along like zombies, never growing but never collapsing. What literature I could find to explain how startups could be more successful reminded me of cookbooks: "Stick to your business plan," "Keep your investors happy by giving them information," "Get to know your customers," and "Be good to your employees."

The curious economist in me kept looking for answers. While still running my company, I took an unpaid part-time post as entrepreneur-in-residence at a university business school. Students seeking my advice told me what they'd been taught about becoming an entrepreneur: in a nutshell, it was to write a business plan and sell your idea to a venture capitalist. This didn't reflect either my own rocky road or the paths that I knew successful entrepreneurs had taken, a conundrum that I discussed at length with the school's dean and other entrepreneurs. So, when the opportunity arose, I couldn't resist the chance to go back to my research roots and attempt to discern the empirical facts about what makes a startup prosper and grow.

At the Kauffman Foundation, as well as through past and subsequent experiences, I had the extraordinary privilege of meeting and learning from thousands of entrepreneurs. In every interaction, I've asked what they learned in the process of creating their ideas and starting their companies. What were the most valuable lessons that they'd gleaned from their successes and from their setbacks and failures?

The stories were of unexpected twists and turns, of vanishing customers, slammed doors, financing roadblocks, being beaten to the punch by another entrepreneur, and being swatted away by skeptical so-called experts, not to mention cheap eating, disapproving in-laws, missed ballet recitals, foregone vacations, and, of course, those sleepless nights. I also heard accounts that began with, "If I'd known then what I know now . . ." and of serendipitous decisions that somehow snatched success from certain failure. I also learned from my own successes, failures, inspirations, and frustrations.

What follows is distilled from the themes recounted by many of these experienced, successful entrepreneurs.

## 1. You Can Learn Only by Doing

Ewing Kauffman, whose fortune endowed his eponymous foundation, left behind enlightening, personal, and sometimes cryptic writings about building a business. He didn't believe that entrepreneurship could be taught, and he thought that business plans were pretty much bunk. As Kauffman saw it, events that appeared critical to success in one company had little relevance to another. When once asked the secrets of starting a successful business, he is reported to have replied, "You have to start a company to learn how to start a company." To put Heraclitus' words in Kauffman's own brand of prose, every startup is different because no entrepreneur steps into the same river as another entrepreneur.

Kauffman started one of history's most successful drug companies by understanding that, to successfully break into a mature industry, he would need to take a new approach. His choice was to emphasize sales and relationship building over science and manufacturing. Kauffman saw the mastery of customer relations as critical. While his competitors set up massive research laboratories, Kauffman manufactured new over-the-counter drugs under licenses from other companies. When most of his competitors advertised their nonprescription products directly to patients, Kauffman bypassed consumers and concentrated on hiring and training salesmen to develop trusting personal and professional relationships with doctors, pharmacies, and drug wholesalers.

Like Kauffman, Steve Jobs decided upon a different approach to sales than had his competitors. Instead of selling through authorized retail channels, as do most computer companies, Jobs created his own stores. He believed that Apple could better serve customers, and get a better sense of what they wanted from Apple products, by buying only from him. Through these direct experiences with customers, Jobs learned to make his products user friendly, durable, and beguilingly beautiful. Through his stores, he has made fierce loyalists of his customers, who continue to camp out on sidewalks to buy Apple's newest products the minute that they appear.

Ted Farnsworth, who started one of the first successful TV marketing firms, told me that he believed success for entrepreneurs boiled down to a simple formula: "For any new company there is only one thing to do: devise a new product and just put it out there. Then you can answer the only two questions that count: Are there customers? How much will they pay?" He went on to tell me, "As an entrepreneur, I'm constantly involved in relearning the answers to these questions. For me, experience is the only way to learn."

## 2. Starting a Company Is Not for Kids

How is it that our stereotype of entrepreneurs suggests that, if someone hasn't created a brilliant new company before age thirty, it's unlikely that it will ever happen? This is the "Mozart Myth" of entrepreneurship. It is reinforced every year by one or two entrepreneurs barely out of their teens who create remarkable startups and garner breathless publicity. Stripe, an online payment service founded in 2010, was started by brothers Patrick and John Collison, both of whom dropped out of college and became billionaires in their twenties. This is a great story, and congratulations to them, but the Collisons don't represent the typical story of entrepreneurship, or even the big picture of new product development. Theirs was one of the unicorns or supernovas—beautiful to behold but rare.

Reality, however, is quite different. Data first collected by the Kauffman Foundation shows that about half of all entrepreneurs never went to college in the first place, and most do not start their companies until they are well along in their careers. The average entrepreneur is nearly forty years old when he launches and more than eighty percent of all new companies are started by people over thirty-five.

Not only are most entrepreneurs middle-aged, but entrepreneurs are getting older, and fast. Twenty years ago, people twenty-five to thirty-five started nearly twice as many companies as they do today. Now, more entrepreneurs are between forty-five and fifty-five than any other age group. Interestingly, entrepreneurs over fifty-five now create more companies than those under thirty-five. And, importantly, the probability of success of a new company surviving rises with the age of the entrepreneur.

While most innovations are the products of much older individuals, youthful innovators do enjoy certain distinct advantages in some areas: they are more conversant with cutting-edge technology, and they are not yet burdened by a lifetime of exposure to various cultural norms. A midcareer traveler, for example, probably would have dismissed the idea of spending a night in the spare bedroom of a complete stranger's home. It is difficult to imagine Airbnb being invented by someone over forty.

## 3. You Will Learn More in a Company Than at a College

Every entrepreneur you'll meet in this book, with one exception, worked for an established company before starting his own. Kauffman was a drug salesman, Jobs worked at Atari, and his co-founder, Steve Wozniak, at Hewlett-Packard. The average entrepreneur works for someone else for nearly fifteen years before starting his own business.

Every aspiring entrepreneur should consider spending time working in a big company. It may seem counterintuitive to suggest that a big company can operate as a *de facto* school that pays you to learn. Consider, however, what an employee can see in a large company. How does the business test and manufacture its products? What are the elements of pricing, and how is a marketing plan developed and tested for its effectiveness? How does it organize and pay its workforce and suppliers, comply with legal and regulatory requirements, and assess its needs for equipment and facilities? How has management learned from its mistakes (or maybe not) and pivoted (or maybe not) to meet changes in market forces? How does it innovate?

Some big companies deserve their reputations as clunky bureaucracies, but many others rival our best research universities in producing innovations. Usually, that means that company management has decided that growth must be achieved through innovation, and that innovation either can be produced internally, as a result of a corporate culture that purposefully encourages employee's, or brought in from outside of the company by an entrepreneur, perhaps in the form of a younger and smaller firm purchased by the larger corporation. Shareholders, too, represented by sophisticated fund or money managers, judge companies by their innovation "pipelines" and have the clout to drive innovation by voicing their dissatisfaction with sluggish growth and penalizing companies that don't innovate.

Joseph Schumpeter, the economist who wrote authoritatively about entrepreneurs, long ago identified innovators as threats to big companies. Corporate behemoths—"incumbents," as Schumpeter called them—were so large that their products often defined entire markets, allowing companies to ignore the promise of evolving technology as a means to meet the changing demands of their customers. More nimble startups—the companies that came up with better products, or faster or cheaper ways to make them—were engaged with what Schumpeter called the "creative destruction" of the plodding giants.

Well-known examples of creative destruction include IBM's neardeath experience at the hands of Microsoft and Apple, whose personal computers displaced the mainframe product that was IBM's foundation, and the fate of Blockbuster, which didn't hear the hoofbeats of Netflix approaching from the other side of the hill. Such upheavals helped shape a revolution in management thinking. In the last three decades, big companies have been the source of many cutting-edge technologies, doubling their production of patentable discoveries.

This is one reason that some large companies have embraced startups, sometimes developing symbiotic relationships[1] and seeking out promising innovators.[2] In the 1980s, startups backed by venture-capital investors were thirteen times more likely to go public than to be bought by a large corporation. Today, however, is a mirror image; a venture-backed startup is seven times more likely to be bought by a big company than to go public.

As we will see later on, many entrepreneurs who started their careers in large corporations regarded them as critical to their subsequent success. Most important, they learned the culture of business, how big companies did or did not do a good job of serving their customers, and their customers' continuously changing needs.

## 4. If You Go to College, Choose Your Major Carefully

This is a fact: the only college preparation for aspiring entrepreneurs that holds as much promise as working and learning in a company is majoring in engineering. The number-two major on that list is any of the physical sciences: chemistry, biology, physics, computer science.

The manner in which engineering is taught in universities is focused on how engineers solve real, everyday problems. Student engineers are somewhat like surgical residents, immersed as partners in the process of discovery, working in laboratories with professors to develop and test new and practical ideas. Consider that companies started by the faculty and graduates of MIT alone, engineers and scientists, if measured in terms of aggregate sales, would represent the world's seventeenth largest economy.[3]

Many engineering schools, including Cincinnati, Cornell, Drexel, Georgia Tech, Northeastern, Purdue, and the University of Southern California, have built co-op experiences into their undergraduate curriculums. The model requires students to work full-time in companies at regular intervals while pursuing their degrees. Dean Kamen, perhaps America's most respected inventor, and Mary Barra, the CEO of GM, both were co-op students at Kettering University, which was founded in 1926 as General Motors Tech to train future engineers and executives.

Without reference to personal knowledge and experience, it is the rare entrepreneur who can see a need for a new product, and simultaneously understand how to bring the resources together to respond. To be effective in building a business requires knowledge that can be leveraged to make something new. Without this knowledge, synthesis is impossible. When I was studying Latin in high school, our teacher always reminded us of why we had to endure the horrible task of mastering vocabulary. Declaring, "You can't paint a barn with a dry brush," she reminded us that translation, the *why* of studying Latin, was impossible without knowing what the words meant.

Engineering and science majors also learn how to accurately and concisely articulate their work in written and oral form. These disciplines require that results be documented and processes demonstrated. While most engineers are unlikely to be mistaken for literary giants, their training requires them to develop a clarity in communication that is a significant asset for an entrepreneur.

## 5. Good Companies Don't Happen Overnight

Of course, because of the media-driven narrative of entrepreneurial success, many entrepreneurs dream of starting an Instagram-like company, selling eighteen months after launch to Facebook for $1 billion, or a WhatsApp, for which Facebook paid $19 billion when it was five years old. In fact, nothing could be less like the experience of the average startup. Instead of making their founders rich, you now know that most fail.

As the numbers suggest, formulating a successful startup takes time. When the founders of successful companies look back on their beginnings, the candid ones admit that they didn't really know what they were doing, or where they were headed. This is an important observation as it suggests a different way to look at startups. In reality, every new company exists to search for a product that, developed through iteration and market testing, will achieve scale. While many aspiring entrepreneurs think that starting a company is all about one good idea, in fact, successful entrepreneurs know that their first idea was seldom what made their company successful. Just as in the big company environment, every startup has to constantly and continuously improve its products if it hopes to survive.

Google provides a good example. At first, it foundered in a sea of search engine companies. Many observers didn't give it a chance in the face of Excite, Webcrawler, Altavista, Infoseek, and Yahoo. (Other than Yahoo, do you recognize those names?) It was not until Google's founders, Larry Page and Sergey Brin, hired a professional CEO, Eric Schmidt, who in turn recruited Hal Varian, that the company found a way to make money. As an economics professor at Berkeley, Varian had developed the algorithms that enabled Google to devise targeted advertising. That business competence allowed it to rapidly rise to dominate the search industry.[4]

It took Google seven years to be able to tell a convincing story to public investors. Similarly, many companies that we routinely think of as having enjoyed overnight success took at least ten years to develop what ultimately became their signature products. GoPro was twelve years old before it was in a sufficiently strong position to persuade public investors to back it. Microsoft and Oracle each were eleven, and Amazon was ten. The average company that has sales revenue strong enough to interest public investors to buy its shares, to go public, is fourteen years old.

These examples illustrate the shakey foundation of the build-to-sell premise of much startup planning. Rather than selling stock to the public or being acquired by a big company, most start-ups continue to be owned by their founders long after ten years. From 2006 to 2016, an average of fewer than one hundred companies per year sold stock for the first time. Combine that number with the number of startups that were acquired by large corporations during the same ten-year period—fewer than an average of one thousand a year—and we readily see that the widely anticipated "exit strategy" that is required to be described in every business plan largely is a chimera. It happens to a mere fraction—fewer than .005 percent—of all startups.

This reality contradicts the widely held view that entrepreneurs start and sell companies as quickly as possible, and then move on to become legendary serial entrepreneurs. Few myths about entrepreneurs are quite as false as this one. Most entrepreneurs start one company. If their startups are successful, most founders work at it for the rest of their lives, building companies that provide both income and a means to build personal wealth.

## 6. Venture Capital Is Likely Irrelevant

Perhaps the most commonly cited justification for writing a business plan is that venture capitalists will require it. The assumption is, of course, that every startup needs their money. Because the prevailing narrative tells us that an exit strategy is the focal end point of the business planning exercise, aspirants sometimes joke that venture investors are their "first customers." This initial misperception leads to the equally mistaken view that, if an investor provides capital to a new venture, the business is more likely to succeed. This overemphasis on the importance of venture capital reflects how the experiences of high-tech firms in Silicon Valley have shaped the public vision of the entrepreneur's story. While many of our well-known tech firms could never have reached critical mass without venture backing, only a nominal number of nontech firms ever get, or, in fact, ever need, the support of these professional investors.

Very few nontech startups will ever appeal to venture investors. Altogether, fewer than five hundred startups are backed by major venture funds each year, and a few thousand more receive capital from individual investors, known as "angels." But, even taken together, startups with venture and angel money constitute only a small fraction of all new companies. A 2004 survey of the five hundred fastest-growing firms in the United States revealed that only seven percent, thirty-five companies, ever had a venture investor.[5]

And, also contrary to conventional wisdom, funding from professional investors is no guarantee of success. The chances of a venture-backed startup surviving five years, which is less than fifty percent, is the same as for all new companies, regardless of the source of funds. In some instances, in fact, the interference and demands of active professional stakeholders can be the reason that a startup falters or fails.[6]

Happily, the majority of nontech startups need much less funding than the average $3 million seed investment made by venture funds. The federal government's first official Census of Entrepreneurs, initially sponsored by the Kauffman Foundation, showed that the average startup needs $50,000 in capital.[7] Most entrepreneurs capitalize their startups using savings, including retirement funds. Sixteen percent of all startups rely on personal credit-card debt. Bank loans, secured by the entrepreneur's personal assets, account for another twelve percent of needed capital. Finally, seven percent of entrepreneurs turned to second mortgages on their homes. Once underway, most businesses capitalize themselves, bootstrapping growth by relying on revenues, or turn to banks for loans secured by the growing company's assets.

## 7. Every Startup Has One CEO

When colleges began teaching entrepreneurship in the 1980s, an idea began to take hold that creative synergies would result if individuals crossfertilized their ideas, helping and inspiring one another in a common workplace. As the idea of entrepreneurial incubators developed, the process of starting a company assumed a social dimension. Nowhere is this more evident than in the ubiquitous view that startups are more likely to succeed if there are two or more founders.[8] Paul Graham, an entrepreneur who founded Y Combinator, the most well-known startup accelerator, argues that for an entrepreneur not to have a cofounder is evidence that "no one has confidence in his idea."[9] Other advocates describe the ideal cofounder as a cross between an engineer and therapist, someone who brings needed technical skills and who will provide emotional support when things go badly.[10]

The contemporary idea that better companies emerge when two entrepreneurs join forces reflects a cherry-picking of history, which was perhaps derived from what initially was thought to be the necessary balance and synergy that Steve Jobs and Steve Wozniak brought to starting Apple. Similarly, Gates and his partner, Paul Allen, appeared perfectly matched to start Microsoft. PayPal remarkably had six "cofounders," including Peter Thiel, who later became famous for bankrolling Facebook.

But, a more realistic look at the history of startups shows that every company, even those claiming multiple founders, had just one person who functioned as the "entrepreneur-in-chief." She is the person who sparked the idea, first articulated the vision for the company and brought others together; the person who functions as the company's driving force, without whom the startup never would have happened. Historically, most companies are the work of one person. Nearly all companies incorporated in Delaware, where the preponderance of startups anticipating growth choose to register, are established by one person. George Eastman was the sole force to bring Kodak into being. Edison was the spark for General Electric, and IBM was Thomas Watson's creation. Fifty-six years after the founding of the Procter & Gamble partnership, when the firm became a publicly traded company, William Procter was formally recognized for what he had been all along, the company's CEO. For good reasons, public investors generally wince at the idea of co-CEOs or shared management models; they look to a single manager–decision maker who can be held responsible for a company's operations and results.

Silicon Valley investors, in fact, waffle a bit on their enthusiasm for multiple founders. They know that one-founder companies have proved to be better bets; over a twenty-year longitudinal study, one-founder firms had a substantially higher rate of successful exits that resulted in returns to the venture firms.[11]

Although the idea of cofounders may symbolize happy and productive synergies, the reality is that most venture firms insist on an organization chart that names a "real" chief, the person who has ultimate responsibility for the management and success of the company. General Eisenhower, charged with beating Germany in World War II, was regarded by most as anything but an egotist. In fact, many believed he got the job of Supreme Allied Commander, in charge of all the nations' armies allied against Hitler, because of his diplomatic and modest ways. He took counsel with generals from other countries, several of whom he regarded as smarter and more astute tacticians than himself. But he also knew that winning a war, at least from his position, was not going to get done by reaching consensus at the top. Winning can't be done without everyone working as a team, but deciding where the team is going devolves to one person. Successful companies have successful leaders, usually one each.

Even among today's most sophisticated technical startups, one person is the reason that the company exists. Elon Musk, who also helped to spark PayPal, became a cofounder of Tesla when he rescued a failing company and redesigned the car as well as its production methods. It was Musk who developed a new marketing strategy, and envisioned the public–private partnerships necessary to create recharging facilities all over the country. Today he is the company's CEO and Chairman of its Board.

Like most entrepreneurs, Musk wanted to control his company's destiny. "Working for myself" is the most commonly stated shared motivation across all entrepreneurs in every sector of the economy. Not so incidentally, entrepreneurs appreciate that starting a company is, by its nature, a solitary experience. While startups often appear to be frenzied, highly social endeavors, in the midst of it all most entrepreneurs resonate with the spirit of Alan Sillitoe's novel, *The Loneliness of the Long Distance Runner.* Sillitoe tells the story of an isolated juvenile criminal who discovers himself by competing in marathons, a sport sometimes defined as "running against yourself." Most entrepreneurs recognize the importance of going it alone.[12] Paul Graham, who encourages cofounding on one hand, also suggests that cofounding is risky because the inevitable "fights among founders" can lead to failed startups.[13]

## 8. When You Start a Company, You Are a Boss

Every startup founder discovers that launching his company means that he has become an employer. In fact, one of his first challenges is to recruit talent. Unlike mature businesses in which managers may be able to substitute what are called capital goods (such as factories and equipment, including robots) for workers, most start-ups are relatively labor-intensive enterprises. In the beginning, entrepreneurs need other people to help make their ideas into con-crete products. And, while established larger firms may have the luxury of making an occasional personnel mistake without hurting the organization in a noticeable way, a single hiring mistake can be fatal to a small startup. This reality requires that entrepreneurs learn to effectively manage people, and they must learn quickly.

Most entrepreneurs intuitively understand three useful rules of hiring. As noted, the first is that it is much harder to manage a workforce with cofounders. Problems of shared decision-making usually surface first in the realm of determining what skills are needed and in evaluating employee performance. Personnel dis-putes often become surrogates for larger disagreements relating to the direction of the company.

Second, entrepreneurs often are tempted to hire friends because they presume that they know them well. One of the most troubling discoveries for new CEOs is understanding that they don't neces-sarily know their friends outside of the context of friendship, and that employment relationships, unlike friendships, can never be equilateral. Because the CEO has the power to fire every employee, she is not the coequal of any employee. While many startups ap-pear to be marvelously friendly, informal, nonhierarchical organi-zations, the CEO, who carries more risk and worry than any other worker, knows that the company's welfare must be her highest pri-ority. When an employee who was first a friend is no longer of stra-tegic value to the company, a firing almost always means the end of the friendship. Don't hire friends—or, even worse, relatives—in the first place.

Third, unless it is unavoidable, it is a mistake to use company ownership—such as shares, options, or other types of interests in the company—to compensate employees. Because every startup that is striving for its scale opportunity is in a continuous state of flux, the relative value of every employee, one to the other, is constantly evolving. In startup companies, if ownership interests have been permanently vested in individuals who, over time, prove to be of less value to the evolving company, the presence of previously granted shares can severely limit the company's flexibility in negotiating with potential investors, and even complicate the hiring of new employees needed for new endeavors. Some entrepreneurs who have been ill-advisedly generous with equity awards have found themselves in messy battles for ownership control, which almost certainly is the beginning of a death spiral for a young company. If employee equity grants can't be avoided, this is the time to spend money on an experienced lawyer who can structure awards in a manner that provides maximum flexibility for the owner.

## 9. Sales Are Everything

Jeff Sandefer, who built a successful oil and gas business, runs the Acton School of Business, the only school in the U.S. that is dedicated solely to teaching entrepreneurs, and the only school that focuses on a sales and marketing, rather than a theoretical, approach.[14] Unlike accelerators owned by wealthy investors who are looking for promising new businesses, Sandefer does not invest in his students' companies, does not profit from running his school, and refunds tuition if a student doesn't succeed as an entrepreneur. Operating a tuition-supported school, with a customer-satisfaction ethos, is apparent in his money-back guarantee, Sandefer keeps careful track of his graduates. Follow-up statistics indicate that his approach to entrepreneurship seems to be paying off. Sixty-three percent of Acton graduates start companies. Most wait nearly two years after graduating to throw the switch, time spent in additional research and development, including extensive testing of the target markets for their innovations.

Sandefer requires that every candidate spend three months selling door-to-door before he may matriculate. Knives, vacuum cleaners, frozen meat—it doesn't matter. The experience makes an aspiring entrepreneur understand what salespeople know: Selling is hard work. There are very few products that sell themselves; every product needs pushing. Selling, for an entrepreneur-in-training, is also the best way to learn how to improve new products. We see that lesson in the sales model that Jobs constructed for Apple: Talking and carefully listening to customers can guide product design and improvement, and successful customer input can drive sales.

Customers control the future of your startup. On more than one occasion, I've heard a failed entrepreneur say that his idea was "ahead of its time," in other words, blaming the customers that he never had. Customers know what they want or need or like, and they will let you know what they find valuable. A corollary lesson about customer demand is to consider whether you are looking in the right place for your market. Recall the earlier story of my first business venture, where I was sure that hospitals would rush to buy my useful healthcare costs and outcomes information, but didn't? How could they be so dumb? When I found the real customers—hospital bond underwriters—who needed the information and were ready to pay for it, I found the market that made the business a success.

## 10. You Need a "Cold Circle"

Everyone wants to cheer on an aspiring entrepreneur. Like the refrain in the old cowboy song, "Home on the Range," "Where never is heard a discouraging word . . ." family members, friends, and kindly advisers are less likely than strangers to tell you the unvarnished truth. Your friends and family want you to succeed and will be reluctant to dampen your aspirations with tough questions. Even if they think that your idea is flat-out bad, they are unlikely to want to damage your relationship by saying so. Perhaps you'll manage to succeed anyway, they may think, and I won't have been the bearer of bad news.

Billy Mann, a songwriter about whom you'll read later, knows that asking a group of friends about your new song is a waste of time. "They will always tell you it's the best you've ever written. Friends and family members are so caught up in your aspirations that they can't really listen critically. They already think you are talented; whatever you write must be great. Their feedback is one-hundred-percent useless in judging how the market might react."

Making the same point, Chile's former economic minister, Carlos Matus, referred to family, friends, and cabinet member colleagues as his "hot circle," a very useful group for support and succor. Matus wisely took great care to test his ideas with a "cold circle" for unbiased input. It is tough to hear skeptical views of what you want to believe is a great idea, but a cold circle can save you a lot of time, pain, and money.

## 11. Making Money Is What It's About

Richard Branson, the founder of Virgin Atlantic Airways and numerous other Virgin enterprises, once defined an entrepreneur as "Someone who jumps off a cliff and builds an airplane on the way down." Every entrepreneur understands this metaphor in very personal terms. Starting a company involves disturbing a career path, risking savings, living with debt, and suffering the possibility that family and friends will see you fail. Attempting to wrestle an idea into a successful business requires psychological fortitude. Not everyone is suited to the uncertainty, sacrifices, and loneliness that typifies the long period from startup to knowing whether a business will succeed.

This is why making money plays such a motivational role for entrepreneurs. If you are not starting a business to make money, go home. Making money is critical to the survival, much less growth, of your company, and pushing forward to achieve scale is the formula for financial success. Would you found a company if you didn't see the potential to grab the golden ring?

Of course, in addition to wanting to make money, many entrepreneurs are animated by nonmonetary or psychological rewards. Imagine the enormous satisfaction of starting a drug company that produces a medicine to cure a terrible disease. Many entrepreneurs, among them Bill Gates, report that one of the greatest rewards in starting a business has been to create jobs. All successful entrepreneurs will tell you that, had they passed by their opportunity to start a company, they would have regretted it for the rest of their lives.

Making money is seen by many as a questionable career goal, venal and self-serving. In the 1987 film *Wall Street*, Michael Douglas' deal-making character Gordon Gekko famously says, "Greed, for lack of a better word, is good." That snatch of film footage continues to resonate as a misleading portrayal of what constitutes "business." Partly as a reaction, interest in "social entrepreneurship" has led to the formation of tens of thousands of not-for-profit organizations, many now referred to as nongovernment organizations or NGOs.[15] Most of these organizations exist to provide what in the past would have been called a charitable service to people too poor to fully participate in the marketplace. Not surprisingly, failure rates for social entrepreneurs are very high.

Many entrepreneurs who have become part of a local ecosystem face a second distraction to their goal of making money. You are not starting a company to revive the local economy. Many colleges, especially in rust-belt cities, encourage entrepreneurship among their students as evidence of the institution's commitment to helping its hometown. Similarly, many cities support business incubators in hopes that entrepreneurs who create businesses while working in them will add to the commercial base of the city. The job of getting a startup underway is hard enough without taking on the task of rekindling the economy around you. No entrepreneur should feel obligated to revive a local economy; her job is to get a business started that will attain scale growth and to maximize its likely success. What if achieving these milestones requires relocating to another city? Big businesses move to maximize efficiency; so should startups.

## 12. If Opportunity Doesn't Knock, Build Your Own Door

Every successful entrepreneur can point to one or two lucky incidents that shaped his success. Formal business plans never mention luck, for good reason. No one can teach you how to maximize good luck or avoid a bad turn of events.

How do entrepreneurs get to be in the right place at the right time? Thomas Jefferson is alleged to have suggested an answer. "I am a great believer in luck and I find the harder I work the more I have of it." For entrepreneurs, good luck is a return on three kinds of hard work. First, the ability to create an innovation relates to the breadth of facts at your command. The more you know, the more creatively you can think. Louis Pasteur's observation about scientific discovery applies equally to entrepreneurs: "Fortune favors the prepared mind."

Second, entrepreneurs, must be effective at building valuable social networks. The more encompassing their web of relationships, the more likely it will produce new opportunities and lead to new ideas, better employees, and more sales. An analog of this rule explains one feature of labor markets. Most people who get a job on the basis of word of mouth, not being recruited or applying for work, benefit from the referral not of a close friend but someone in a more remote second or third circle of acquaintances.

Third, good luck involves making opportunity from accidents. Everyday occurrences, a new twist on a product design, or a comment made by a customer on a sales call, may open an unexpected door. Entrepreneurs must make their own luck or, as the comedian Milton Berle once advised, "If opportunity doesn't knock, build a door."

Being familiar with these twelve perspectives on what every entrepreneur should know will help you find more value in what follows. These lessons do not serve as a formula for success in which each operates as a critical ingredient. In all likelihood it will be only after the fact that you will recognize which were most important to your experience. Without such experience, however, these elements, considered together, may help you understand the task of becoming a successful entrepreneur—and whether what's required of you seems authentic to your aspirations.

# CHAPTER 3

# Why Start a Company?

Every morning, the trellised parking lot at the Kauffman Foundation shook with the roar of an incoming Harley-Davidson Road King, a real hog. The manager of our mailroom had arrived for work. Dan defied the stereotype of a biker: no leather jacket, no tattoos, and no scraggly beard. He was a quiet professional, a model employee who had worked at the Foundation almost from its inception ten years earlier.

Dan's passion was working on motorcycle engines. He enjoyed a reputation for being able to fix the tough problems that most professional mechanics couldn't solve. One day, after we had worked together for three years, Dan came to talk with me about something exciting. After years of working on bikes, he had become exasperated with the way that many engines were designed. His chief irritation was that it was almost impossible to access some critical engine parts for routine cleaning without taking apart much of the motor. To solve this problem, he had invented an articulated wrench that allowed a mechanic to access inner areas of the motorcycle motor, unbolt hard-to-reach parts, and extract them for servicing. Dan had filed a patent application for his wrench, and two other tools as well. He had a local foundry produce the parts and then assembled them in his garage. Word of mouth had spread the news of his innovation, and he now was shipping wrenches to bikers all over the world.

When Dan told me that he was leaving his Foundation job to start a company, I asked if he was sure that he wanted to give up the security of his steady employment. He was in his forties and had a family. Smiling broadly, he told me that his wrench sales already almost matched his Kauffman salary, and that his wife, who also had a good job, was encouraging him to devote full time to his hobby-business. Like many entrepreneurs, Dan saw nothing but blue skies ahead. In his case, it seemed justified; he had a growing business and customers who were showing enthusiastic demand for his unique products.

Dan's news came as a surprise to everyone. No one had suspected his secret life as an innovating toolmaker who would morph into an entrepreneur. He worked in the belly of the beast of entrepreneurship, but had never revealed any particular interest in our mission nor had he used our library, which included the biographies of hundreds of entrepreneurs and reams of material on startups. Over his years at the Foundation, Dan had shipped out thousands of books on the process of business formation, but never thought that he might need to read one. He said he was surprised to discover that he was an entrepreneur; as he saw it, all he had done was to apply his common sense to a problem that cost him, and other mechanics, a lot of time and aggravation.

How did Dan's idea turn him into an entrepreneur, one secure enough to leave a steady job to set sail for motorcycle-tool success? What motivates anyone to take the risks and persevere to build a successful company? My years of interactions with entrepreneurs showed me the fascinating array of reasons and circumstances that have catalyzed various individuals into action. These individuals, and their motivations, seem as different one from the other as are the enterprises that resulted.

## This Idea Will Make the World Better, and It's Mine

Dan discovered that his identity was more rooted in his passion for motorcycle mechanics than his capable management of our mailroom. By tinkering to resolve his own bike's problems, he realized that he had solved the same problem for thousands of others. If his idea was to be of any benefit to his fellow bike enthusiasts, though, he had to figure out how to tell them about it. This is a great example of how many entrepreneurs come to deeply love their ideas, much as they would a child who requires their stewardship. They develop a sense of responsibility for the idea, and a sense of obligation to those who could benefit from it, to nurture, develop, and share. In short, they know that if they don't put this out where others can benefit from it, they will be wasting an opportunity to help.

A wry corollary to this sense of responsibility and obligation, which I've heard time and again, is a fairly common spectral nightmare. This dream has many variations, but the gist of it is that someone comes along, just a few months or years later, and has built a product that is similar but inferior to what the aspiring innovator had laid to the side in favor of safety and security. This surreal nightmare plays out in imagined media stories, YouTube product demonstrations, and fantastic sales reports that go viral on the Internet, while the "But That Was My Idea!" salary man shouts at the computer screen. The moral of the story is that many entrepreneurs are motivated to succeed by the fear of being inconsequential when they had dreamed of better.

## Business Is My Creative Outlet

College students, including those studying entrepreneurship, live in an environment that celebrates creative people—thought of as those who make movies, paint, compose music, design buildings, or write novels and poetry. The most intriguing are those who make lots of money and become famous in the process, which may explain the astonishing number of film majors in universities across America.

Yet, data clearly shows that most college graduates spend their lives in the business side of the world, even when the underlying nature of the business, whether in a small landscaping company or a large fabric manufacturer, is a creative enterprise. Why does our culture limit the application of the creative label to the arts, but doesn't apply it to innovators who develop ground-breaking ideas—for Invisalign braces, cordless screwdrivers, vacuum food packaging, and electronic textbook rental—and who then figure out a way to bring those innovations to the market? The development of thousands of new products and services that make our lives and work more efficient, convenient, safe, and pleasurable, and the business systems that get those products and services to us, is a creative art form.

One very successful entrepreneur's story is a perfect example of the intersection and synthesis of artistic and business acumen. Billy Mann grew up in a poor Philadelphia neighborhood. To pay for college, he worked in the cafeteria by day and operated the school's old-fashioned manual switchboard at night. Hoping to become a songwriter, Mann majored in music, although he realized that his chances of becoming an income-generating composer were infinitesimal. His mother thought so, too, and pushed him to go to law school. But Mann couldn't let go of his dream of writing songs. To mollify his mother and settle his dilemma, he gave himself a year to make it in the entertainment world. If he flopped, he promised his mother that he'd take the LSAT and move on.

After graduation, Mann set out for California. He drove his old Nissan Sentra, taking two months to make it across the country. He worked odd jobs along the way to pay for gas and food. Once he'd made it to San Francisco, Mann got a job at a futon store. A few weeks later, he fell asleep at work while "testing" the product and was fired.

Flat broke, Mann took his guitar to Fisherman's Wharf to busk for money. He made less than eight dollars on his first day, not nearly enough to eat or pay the rent that was due in two weeks. Early the next morning, he was riffing on his guitar when a new-lywed couple strolled by. He was talking them up when he had an inspiration. "If I compose a song about you in the next five minutes, will you give me five dollars?" On the spot, he invented a sweet song about where the couple had grown up, how they had met and fallen in love, and how happy their future would be. Delighted, the couple gave him ten dollars.

Mann realized that Fisherman's Wharf was a favorite spot for honeymooning couples, so he spent the next day plucking at their heartstrings, improvising custom songs. By evening, he had made $318. Mann told me, "That was the moment that I became an entre-preneur. I saw the entrepreneurial matrix in 3D and knew I could integrate my passion for music into my working life."

Making a living on the street was tough and unpredictable work. Mann gradually moved on to make a subsistence income playing in bars and clubs, where he sang hit songs on request. "I knew I could write better songs than what people were listening to," he says. He began using his club gigs to try out his own compositions. Once in a while he sold a song to a record company. The contracts provided a bit of money up front and promised royalties that never seemed to materialize. Mann was slowly sinking. Just as he was about to give up and head back east to law school, a royalty check for $136,000 arrived in the mail.

That windfall settled the matter: Mann would stick with songwriting. He started composing more and better songs, but quickly realized that he also needed to understand the complex ins and outs of the music publishing and marketing world. Within five years of his first ten-dollar gig at Fisherman's Wharf, Céline Dion sang two of Mann's songs, including the title song of her platinum-selling album, *Let's Talk About Love*.

But Mann still couldn't interest a major record label in his songs. He decided that the only way to break through was to make his own albums. Then, as his reputation grew in the music industry, he found himself arranging extra gigs for vocalists and band members, all good friends, who he had employed at his recording studio. At one point, his lawyer pointed out that every time Mann sent one of his pals out to a gig, it was their agents, not Mann, getting paid. Mann took on the job of representing talent, eventually building Stealth, a New York talent agency, and garnering P!nk, Art Garfunkel, Jessica Simpson, Sheryl Crow, Justin Timberlake, and the Backstreet Boys as clients.

In 2007, Mann sold his company to EMI, one of the world's biggest entertainment companies, which had recorded the Beatles in its famous Abbey Road studios. He moved to London and eventually became president of EMI's record division. When EMI was sold in 2012, Mann returned to the United States and started another talent agency. He hadn't lost his touch: Among the winners on Grammy night 2015 were Sam Smith, Meghan Trainor, and Maroon 5, all part of Mann's network.

When I asked Mann what he had learned about being an entrepreneur, he boiled it down to a five-word formula: "First, create; second, be judged." He explained, "There is no way you know anything new is good until you test it in the market."

---

As an entrepreneur, Mann is pushing the frontier of the entertainment business. His own experiences led him to wonder how many talented artists remain undiscovered because of the difficulty of breaking into big complex media companies. Mann believes that there are lots of star performers out there, but that many go unrecognized because gaining the attention of record companies involves convoluted steps such as making expensive demo tapes and desperately scrambling for auditions.

In 2014, Mann met Jacob Whitesides, a talented young songwriter and singer. No matter how hard Jacob had tried, he couldn't get an audition with a major label. Mann was inspired by Whitesides' frustrating experience and urged him to try a new approach, which Mann called "busking on the Internet." He developed a strategy that enabled Whitesides to bypass corporate gatekeepers and go directly to the market to leverage social media. In February 2015, following Mann's roadmap, Whitesides released a new song, "A Piece of Me," which he promoted with an Internet-only campaign. It shot into the iTunes Top 10 and rose to number five on the Billboard charts. Mann proudly told me that Whitesides, "along with his fan base, had given himself a record deal."

One evening, while I talked with Mann over dinner in Mexico, he quietly observed that he couldn't determine which of the two parts of his life, music or business, required more creativity. What Mann did was to bring the full force of his creative talent, including some talents that he didn't know he had, to his work of writing music, managing a recording studio, and bringing other artists to the attention of the world through innovative vectors. For Mann, forging new paths in the entertainment business has provided its own creative rewards.

• • •

Solomon Snyder, who is widely recognized as the most productive brain biologist in the world, illustrates the confluence of creativity and business. Snyder, for whom Johns Hopkins named its department of neuroscience, is famous for many discoveries including how proteins on the surface of specific brain cells act as neuroreceptors for specific drugs. The technology he subsequently devised to do high-speed testing of the reaction between an infinite number of chemical agents and millions of types of brain cells, led to the creation of two drug-discovery companies, and many new drugs.

Snyder once told me that business provided him with an environment in which he could accelerate the invention of new drugs, moving faster and with more freedom than university research culture allows and leveraging his talent in ways that would be of most value to many more patients. Once he had ingeniously routinized the drug-discovery process, he was able to focus his research on exploring whole new frontiers of brain science. Subsequently, Snyder discovered the presence of gases in the brain, something scientific consensus previously had believed was impossible. In time, the discovery of the chemistry for Viagra confirmed Snyder's discovery that nitrous oxide in the brain could signal the body to increase blood flow to specific organs.

## I Want to Be the Boss of Me

Research tells us that, at some point in their lives and for however short-lived a time, most people aspire to launching their own companies and working for themselves. As we have seen, more than 90 percent of entrepreneurs spend their early working years in the employ of someone else. When an idea begins to form, however, some employees decide to start their own companies as the means to take control over their lives, to do things differently and better as a boss, and to work with an inspired purpose.

Peckham Library
Please remember to save your receipt to collect your Reader Reward points.
Reader Reward Points = Free DVD Rentals!

**Customer ID: *******3638**

**Items that you renewed**

Title: Burn the business plan : what great entrepreneurs really do
**Due: 27/12/2018  23:59**

Total items: 1
05/12/2018 12:29
Checked out: 1
Overdue: 0


Thank you for visiting Southwark Libraries

When he was growing up, it would have been impossible to guess that Ewing Kauffman would start a major pharmaceutical company. He was born on a Kansas farm in 1916. His father was missing most of the time and his mother, to make ends meet, moved to Kansas City to run a boarding house. Kauffman was ill and bedridden for part of his childhood, a period during which he became a voracious reader and taught himself to do complex math problems in his head.

Before Kauffman could realize his dream of going to college, he was drafted into the Navy during World War II. When the Navy assessed him to have quantitative skills, he was trained to be a ship's navigator. In his off-duty hours, Kauffman's math acumen came in handy in other ways: He played poker so well that he earned the nickname "Lucky."

One night, while serving on the flagship of a large convoy carrying much-needed oil from South America to U.S. refineries, Seaman Kauffman came to doubt the calculations set by the chief navigator, an officer. He was convinced that all twenty ships were heading out of a deep-ocean shipping lane and would soon be dangerously close to shoals, which would surely lead to disaster.

Kauffman knew that he could verify his fix on their true position by using maps of ocean depths, but to do so he would have to use the ship's sonar. This was forbidden; German submarines were thought to be in the area and, if they heard the distinctive bounceback ping of the sonar, the next sound that anyone in the convoy would hear would be the whine of German torpedoes. But when Kauffman's superiors dismissed his pleas to reconsider their calculations, Kauffman knew that he had to do something.

In desperation, he activated the sonar and sent one ping to the bottom, which confirmed his theory about the convoy's true position. Then, breaking the chain of command, he awakened the captain by pounding on his cabin door. The irate commanding officer

greeted this insubordination by loudly announcing that, if Kauffman was wrong, he would be court-martialed. Lucky for "Lucky,"
his calculations were spot-on and a catastrophic accident was
averted. Later that night, the captain promoted Kauffman.

When Kauffman returned home to Kansas City, he brought his
luck and dogged determination, and his poker winnings, with him.
He took a job as a "detail man," a pharmaceuticals salesman who
visited doctors to persuade them of the benefits of a company's
products. It was clear from the outset that Kauffman had a flair for
selling; in his first year, his commission income exceeded the company president's salary. The CEO's response was to cut Kauffman's
territory. The following year, with fewer doctors to visit, Kauffman
again outearned the president. This time, the CEO cheated him
by changing the commission formula. Kauffman quit on the spot
and vowed never to work for anyone else again. He was perfectly
primed for an entrepreneurial moment. All that was missing was a
good idea.

Kauffman returned to visit many of the doctors whom he'd
met in Kansas and Missouri to ask what kinds of compounds they
needed for their patients but weren't able to obtain. The postwar
baby boom was in full swing, and many doctors expressed concern
that they were seeing too many low-birth-weight babies, a problem
that they thought might be prevented if pregnant women had more
calcium in their diets. Happily, Kauffman realized that creating calcium tablets would not require years of research in a pharmaceutical laboratory; all he had to do was figure out how to make them.

Working in his basement at night, Kauffman scraped out the
insides of oyster shells that had been discarded by Kansas City
restaurants, harvesting their calcium. He reduced the scrapings to
a fine powder and pressed it into pills. By day, Kauffman was his
own detail man, crisscrossing the region to showcase his calcium
pills to doctors, who then recommended them to their pregnant pa-

tients. Because he wanted it to appear that his product was made by an established company and not by his one-man basement operation, Kauffman's business cards announced that he was a representative of Marion Laboratories. Marion was his mother's name.

With his calcium tablets, Kauffman had invented a new kind of pharmaceutical company, one that was focused primarily on customer need and sales and not on developing products in research laboratories. When he decided to leverage the distribution system that he had built for his signature over-the-counter calcium drug, OsCal, to sell prescription pharmaceuticals, Kauffman again abjured the traditional route; instead of building expensive lab facilities, he licensed new formulas from university researchers and foreign pharmaceutical companies.

Kauffman's real genius was his ability to inspire a sales force. He created innovative incentive systems, famously awarding light blue convertibles—Chevrolets at first, then Cadillacs when the company became more profitable—to his standout salesmen. Kauffman truly believed, and made his employees truly believe, that they were doing doctors and pharmacists an important service by providing the products that would help their patients return to good health.

Kauffman was always looking for new ideas to improve sales. One was to use brightly colored labels for all of Marion Labs' products instead of the industry standard white label. Pharmacists reported that the distinctive labels made it easier to find the company's products on their shelves when filling generic prescriptions, which helped Marion Labs outpace its competitors.

Kauffman also was famous for being a good boss, perhaps because he had experienced the frustration of bad bosses who denigrated commitment and talent. He often announced that any smart boss should hire people who were even smarter, and should value their contributions. Marion Labs paid well and provided generous benefits, including a profit-sharing plan and stock options. When the company went public, hundreds of his employees became millionaires.

## There's a Better Way to Do This

Shortly after I became president of the Kauffman Foundation, *Fortune* magazine published a cover story titled "Overcoming Dyslexia," which described how many revolutionary companies had been started by people who described themselves as dyslexic.[1] The cover featured photos of John Chambers of Cisco, Charles Schwab, who invented the discount brokerage concept, and Ted Turner, who founded CNN and supercharged the nascent cable TV industry. Richard Branson also was pictured. The story told how Branson considered starting his own business because he was so awful in school. He was quoted as saying, "Look, if I'd been good at math, I probably never would have started an airline." The many entrepreneurs who may be dyslexic include those who started their companies in their late twenties and early thirties, much earlier than most other startup founders. These entrepreneurs seem particularly eager to create companies that approach problem solving in a new way and in which they could make new, and often unconventional, business decisions.

Prompted by the anecdotal evidence of the *Forbes* article, Kauffman Foundation researchers began to examine the relationship between what we broadly know as dyslexia and entrepreneurship. As we examined the stories of some of America's most famous entrepreneurs, including Alexander Graham Bell, Henry Ford, Thomas Edison, Frank Woolworth, and IBM founder Thomas Watson, we found telltale indications that all of these giants were what we now might call dyslexic, although, of course, at the time, the range of attributes of dyslexia weren't well defined or understood and didn't have a name.

Paul Orfalea, the founder of Kinko's, once described to me the profound problems that he had always had with reading. He came up with the idea of his copying business when he was in school because he had to borrow so many notes from fellow students. Ross Perot, the creator of Electronic Data Systems, who also was featured in the *Fortune* article, was famous for his "one page or less" rule. He hated reading and believed that any idea could be outlined in one page. When I once worked with him on a project, I noticed that providing him a cursory one-page memo would lead to hours of valuable discussion in which Perot would absorb, test, and challenge every idea. A longer document would have gone unread.

To learn whether there was any basis for the observation that dyslexics are disproportionately represented in the ranks of successful entrepreneurs, the Kauffman Foundation commissioned research from several respected scholars. We convened a conference in Phoenix in 2009 to discuss the findings, inviting experts in related fields as well as several successful entrepreneurs who had self-identified as dyslexic.

At that conference, Steve Walker, founder of New England Wood Pellet, related how his experience as a student in a suburban Boston public school had been an endless nightmare. Every day, he said, teachers conveyed how dumb he was. No matter how hard he tried, he couldn't master reading. He never passed a math test. Other students made fun of him for being stupid, a common experience for dyslexic children. The only thing Walker liked about school was shop class, and he fondly remembers his shop teacher as "the only person, and that included my parents, who 'got' me." The shop teacher would often leave the electricity on in the shop area—a violation of school policy—so Walker could use the machinery long into the night. "My shop teacher constantly encouraged me. He said that I could do things that no other student could do."

After squeaking into college and struggling for a year, Walker returned home. One day, he heard that his school had decided to close its wood-and-machine shops and sell the equipment. Walker and his former shop teacher took on the task of selling the machines at an auction. Walker asked his teacher's advice as to which machines he should buy with two thousand dollars, all the money he had. The shop teacher replied with a basic rule of business: "Value is what someone is prepared to pay." As it turned out, no one else even submitted a bid, and Walker was able to buy all of the machines.

Walker set up shop in his basement. The very next week, he was in a hardware store and noticed a display of stoves that burned wood pellets. He wasn't interested in buying a stove, but the adjacent stack of pellet fuel bags, labeled "Made in Montana," caught his eye. Why, he wondered, should people surrounded by the dense forests of the Northeast have to buy wood pellets that had been shipped across the country?

Walker began experimenting in his shop and soon designed and built a machine that compressed sawdust into pellets. His cheaper and better local product was greeted with enthusiasm, and he soon had to build a much bigger machine to keep up with demand. At the time of the Kauffman conference, nineteen years after Walker founded New England Wood Pellet, it was the largest manufacturer of clean, renewable biomass fuel in the Northeast. Among his many achievements, Walker is most proud that his products have displaced millions of barrels of nonrenewable heating oil every year.

According to the results of the Kauffman study, Walker's experience was anything but anomalous. The researchers concluded that about thirty-five percent of all entrepreneurs are dyslexic, substantially higher than the ten percent in the population at large. *Journey into Dyslexia*, an HBO special inspired by the Kauffman conference, explored the reason why dyslexics tend to create more businesses.[2] In 2014, at the first conference of what has become the Dyslexic Entrepreneurs Network, entrepreneurs from around the country came together to compare their histories.[3] Confirming the narrative of the HBO documentary, they shared the belief that they had started their companies to avoid the constraints and rules that they had hated when working for others.

A Johns Hopkins study sheds further light on why a disproportionate share of companies are created by dyslexics. Using a control group study, the researchers compared the careers of men who, as boys, had shown no learning problems, with a group that had experienced serious reading difficulties. Men in the control group had attended a private suburban school, while those in the second group had gone to a school that specialized in teaching boys with learning issues. By the age of forty, the number of boys from the first school who had entered established professions—becoming doctors, lawyers, teachers—was twice that of the boys from the second school. That's not much of a surprise. But, what was startling was that the poor-reader graduates of the second school were three times more likely than their control group counterparts to have started a business.[4] The study concluded that dyslexics, finding it difficult to master the large bodies of settled knowledge and the unremitting testing regimens required to enter established professions, had instead started businesses to create environments in which they could succeed—places where they made the rules. The study also speculated that dyslexic entrepreneurs may be successful because they see innovation opportunities in an intuitive big-picture way. This sense of seeing the world differently is often mentioned by dyslexic adults who have succeeded in environments of their own making; one such entrepreneur—only half-jokingly—refers to this as the "gift of dyslexia."

## Change or Die; My Family's Business Is My Startup

Who would think that a third-generation family-business owner would become an entrepreneur? Heirs sometimes find their inner entrepreneur when they assume the mantle, even if they are reluctant recipients of that responsibility. They may feel burdened by the raft of ancestral expectations that has descended upon them, including a resistance to change the way that things have always been done. What happens when the new-generation manager recognizes that the business has lost its innovative culture and that he must either rescue the enterprise or plan its funeral? A legacy manager may see new opportunities to leverage existing assets, develop innovative products, and may have the inclination to pursue aggressive growth, that is, to treat his legacy like a startup and create a new trajectory.

During the toughest times of the Depression, Carrie Hawkins opened a rural roadside farm stand in upstate New York to help support her family. In 1934, she and her family moved the operation to a busier highway location near their farm. Little did she know that Green Hills Farms—the name of that first little stand—would be the birthplace of a revolution in grocery retailing that would influence grocery stores around the world. In 2001, *Inc.* magazine called Green Hills the "Best Little Store in America."

In the 1990s, Carrie's grandson, Gary Hawkins, feared the opening of major chain grocery stores nearby. Anticipating the fierce competition that a giant supermarket would bring, he began to gather detailed data on his customers at checkout. A self-taught programmer, Hawkins then built analytic software that revealed some unexpected information: About thirty percent of his customers accounted for eighty percent of his profit. Mass coupon mailings and ads in the local newspapers seemed an inefficient way of bonding with this critical segment, which, if lost to the competition, would put him out of business.

Hawkins decided to focus on his best customers, setting out not just to know them by name but to learn about their lives and their families. In time, he knew what they bought, how they responded to sales, and what days of the week they shopped. He was determined to pamper them; at Christmas, he presented beautiful Christmas trees to the top spenders, and once a year he invited them to a black-tie dinner in the store. During a prolonged power failure, he issued special coupons to help customers restock the lost food in their freezers and refrigerators.

Green Hills' customer retention rates and sales per square foot became legend in the industry. In 2011, *Grocery Headquarters*, the industry's leading publication, voted Hawkins its retail executive of the year, a remarkable achievement for a one-store owner. Customer loyalty programs are now such a part of our lives that it is hard to imagine that the model was developed so recently, and in a little store outside Syracuse.

Hawkins' innovation saved the family business. Actually, it changed the store's future, and Hawkins' future as well. After he received the grocery industry award, stores all over the world began to ask Hawkins for advice. The demand was so strong that he decided to create a new company to manage customer data and loyalty programs. Now Hawkins is the CEO of the advisory company that he founded in 2010, the Center for Advanced Retailing and Technology (CART). CART now advises retailers worldwide, including Unilever and Procter & Gamble.

## Don't Start a Business So That You Can Be Called an Entrepreneur (and Get Rich Quick)

In the past thirty years, it has become increasingly fashionable to be known by others as an entrepreneur. This reflects a changed environment in how business innovators are viewed in contemporary culture, one that reflects the changing nature of technology itself. The entrepreneurs of the turn of the nineteenth century, often called "captains of industry," magnates, and tycoons, leveraged the emerging technologies of the industrial revolution to build giant companies in industries like steel, oil, and railroading. Many, including Andrew Carnegie, Henry Frick, Hollis Collins, Jay Gould, and, of course, John D. Rockefeller, were labeled robber barons and, despite their wealth, philanthropy, and high social standing, were widely despised.

By contrast, today's wealthy and socially prominent entrepreneurs generally are admired by the public and are the frequent subjects of laudatory media narratives. No one sees them as the near criminals that their counterparts of one hundred years ago were made out to be. Why is that?

Colleges and universities have both participated in and championed this positive perception by characterizing "entrepreneur" as a vocation—like physician, computer programmer, chemist, or accountant. Institutions do this, in part, by offering what looks like a regular course of study or path to becoming a successful entrepreneur. Unfortunately, this is an empty promise: There is no evidence that a student can learn how to start a business in much the same manner that he can train to be an architect or a zoologist.

The students on this academic and career track may be thought of as *wannapreneurs*. They hope to become another Zuckerberg, even though most know little more about him than that he started

Facebook and became very rich. While achieving financial success certainly is a part of every entrepreneur's motivation, in part because it symbolizes the belief that society values what you have to offer, we know that entrepreneurs who start companies with the *primary goal* of making money have a much higher failure rate. In pursuit of quick money, wannapreneurs discount the long-run economic return of building a lasting company.

At a conference several years ago, I met a student; let's call him Jared. He was determined to become an entrepreneur. A few years later, Jared contacted me to report that he indeed had become an Internet mattress sales entrepreneur, and asked for my thoughts. It was odd, I recall thinking, but I'd been asked for advice on the subject of mattresses several other times in the previous year. A little research revealed that an increasing proportion of mattress sales were occurring in e-commerce, a far cry from the remembered days of trying out mattresses—firm? extra firm? medium?—and being a little creeped out by thoughts of the hygiene standards of previous shoppers. What had caused this surge of interest in mattresses entrepreneurship? Did the population's pursuit of a good night's sleep hold boundless potential? Had I not noticed that mattress stores were dropping like flies?

When Jared called, I asked how he had come to his interest in mattresses and how he was dealing with what looked to be a lot of competition, given the approximately 9,000 mattress stores in the United States alone. Comparatively, there are only about 12,000 Starbucks stores. As buying a cup of coffee is an everyday ritual for many, abundant locations make sense, but mattresses often are a once in a decade purchase. Jared's answer about his idea's inception was interesting. He told me that he had attended a meeting organized by the White House to encourage recent college graduates to start businesses. At that meeting, a Small Business Administration official had read a list of hot new industries that the attendees should consider. Mattresses were on the list.

Jared thought that this sounded like a promising idea. He did some additional research and decided that, while others in the business were targeting newlyweds, new homeowners, and couples who had kids, he would aim for the dorm market. He was building a marketing business aimed at college students, outsourcing production and drop-shipping to customers.

Some of Jared's family members had invested in his business. His relatives, he said, were impressed with his vision. When I asked what they had found intriguing he responded, "This business is all about building the exit." Jared is betting that, if he can capture even a modest part of the student market, a big mattress company will buy him out for a lot of money.

Jared's motivation was to be an entrepreneur and make a lot of money. Most previous generations of startup founders, even the most recent crops of successful entrepreneurs, came at this from the other end: first, they had the business idea (often one about which they were passionate), and then they formed the business. Instead, Jared had decided to form a business and then to look for a business idea, but only a business idea that would permit him a profitable exit in a relatively short time. Assuredly, Jared did not profess any passion for mattresses; he is not driven by his unique expertise or an innovative idea, and he is building a business not to last but to create a reasonably successful and quickly saleable company.

I wish Jared nothing but the best. I hope that his plan works and that he makes a bundle of money. But the odds are not in his favor. First, he is pursuing a business opportunity that was identified by the government, which is not such a good idea. In examining decades of government forecasting, economists have learned that government's predictive conclusions as to which new industries will grow, and where the most promising occupational opportunities exist, have been rather notoriously and consistently wrong.[5] Research on startup success rates tells us something even more important, however: failure rates are considerably higher for companies that are started with the intention of a short-term sale.

Jared might have something to learn from Dan the motorcycle-wrench inventor, Billy Mann, Ewing Kauffman, Steve Walker, and Gary Hawkins. While each was motivated to make his startup financially successful, none were solely or even principally motivated by that quest. Rather, starting and building their companies offered them, variously, a chance to make useful products that solved real problems, a fulfilling creative talent, a place to run a company as a boss, and the challenge of growing a legacy business into an innovative and prosperous company. And, of course, they also knew that if they got it right and had a little luck, they might reap significant financial rewards.

# CHAPTER 4

# What Motivates Entrepreneurs?

Every fall brings certain rituals to college campuses. If the university teaches civil engineering, groups of students will appear on the quad with transits, measuring tapes, and notebooks. Over the years, thousands of students have established for themselves the exact elevation from sea level of the threshold of the engineering building, and precisely how far it is from there to the bottom step of the chapel stairs.

If the school teaches entrepreneurship, another group of students can be seen walking around, intently peering at everything from the delivery bags used by campus pizza vendors to the tennis courts, wondering if a phone app could more efficiently manage athletic facility reservations. Those students have been charged by their professors to find problems in the world around them that suggest the need for new businesses. Entrepreneurship textbooks call this *opportunity recognition*. Every student about to write a business plan for an entrepreneurship course is taught that new companies are built on fulfilling unique, previously unmet needs, and students' plans must articulate the new business opportunities that they have recognized.

Professors grading their students' plans throughout the semester will encounter ideas that they will have seen dozens of times before. Typical examples include turning leftover cafeteria food into pet treats, using drones to optimize campus parking spots at different times of the day, and starting a "real" orientation website for new students that contains information that the administration doesn't necessarily want new students to know, for example, bars that don't "card" students. Ideas for businesses built on new apps recycle as well: tracking calorie consumption, using games to teach physics, efficiently distributing vaccines in the African bush, and real-time assessment of the wait time at a local take-out restaurant.

Seldom do new business ideas emerge from this process. Students can no more innovate on demand than anyone else. The picture of students walking around on their first day of entrepreneurship class, desperately looking for a business opportunity, tells us a lot about why colleges fail at teaching entrepreneurship. If we can't understand how real innovation happens, how can we teach it?

Creating a new product or service is an organic process, one that is shaped by the background, experience, and acuity of the innovator, as well as his inclination to see that solving a problem is necessary or useful and that the solution is marketable. And, of course, the creation of a new business is determined by the perseverance of the entrepreneur.

## Who Innovates and Why?

Few successful companies are started as a result of a purposeful search for an opportunity. Most result from the recognition of a real problem, the curiosity to seek an answer and—most often but not always—an existing skill set that informs a possible solution. Whether an entrepreneur invents a new product, buys a franchise, or takes over an existing business, she ideally will be creating a better and more efficient way to get a product or service to customers. Innovation, the creation of new or improved solutions or tools to solve existing or emergent needs, is a process linked both to the state of existing technology and to an individual's proclivity to recognize an opportunity and invent a solution.

It's a given that existing product and service breakthroughs shape the evolution of subsequent innovation. What is not so clear is how that constant evolution enables more innovation in the hands of more people. You can envision the bicycle as a symbol of a transformative leap of enormous importance in and of itself— and also as one that became even more important as a tool that enabled and accelerated innovation in many areas that obviously were unforeseen by the nameless tinkering mechanics who started it all.

Appearing around 1820, the bike is a brilliant mechanical device that converts human energy into forward motion. The nascent industrial revolution's creation of hard steel made the needed roller chains and sprocket gears possible. Besides the convenience of making the daily trip to the bakery less time-consuming—a miraculous gift of time to those first experiencing it—millions saw their bicycles as tools for discovery. The world beyond a day's walk was suddenly knowable. The bicycle opened new horizons for humankind.

And then along came Henry Ford and the Wright brothers. These geniuses evolved the basic mechanics of the bicycle into new ways to speed travel. Ford's quadricycle was really two bicycles joined by a platform that held a gasoline engine, itself newly developed for other purposes, and had room for a driver. The engine was connected to the vehicle's wheels with bike chains. The Wrights, whose original business was building bicycles, invented the first airplane by mounting a gas engine on a winged airframe, connecting it to propellers with bike chains.

The colossal influence of the bicycle cannot be understated. Today, successive inventions derived from bike technology account for at least one-fifth of the world's economic activity. Steve Jobs said that the bike operated as a metaphor for discovery; he referred to his personal computer as the means to accelerate any user's capacity to learn, describing it as a "bicycle for the mind." Jobs' computers, and the iPhone, iPads, and phone apps that followed have been the genesis of a fast-rushing and endless stream of subsequent innovation.

While all innovation builds on a continuously expanding base of technology, creating new products depends on an individual being qualified by background, and predisposed by curiosity, to take up the challenge of fixing a problem that he sees as worth solving. Thus, innovation is the organic process of an individual applying what came before him to a new problem that he chooses to attack. Innovative entrepreneurs all stand on the shoulders of previous inventors.

To better understand innovators, consider that they are likely to share certain traits. Most are in middle age when they develop solutions that inspire them to form new companies. The average age of an inventor awarded a patent is forty-seven.

The reason? Innovation involves the synthesis of accumulated knowledge, much of it subconscious, that the inventor has absorbed and compiled over his life. The base from which he draws the information is composed of insights acquired through some combination of formal study and training, work experience, and the cognitive challenges that he recognizes, perhaps even in the most mundane of life's tasks: driving, shopping, or paying the phone bill.

The idea of innovators being older is hard to process for some, especially in the narrative of youthful entrepreneurs. Consider, however, that, in most cases, police officers must spend years as beat cops before they are promoted to detective to take on the task of investigating and solving crimes.[1] Detectives have gained experience because they've previously seen a lot, learned a lot about human behavior, and have been in many different difficult and perhaps tragic situations. This idea is revealed in fiction, too; Sherlock Holmes is a mature man; Miss Marple is a beguilingly sweet elderly lady with a razor-sharp mind, honed by a lifetime of observing human frailties.

For a somewhat more rarefied example, consider that the median age of a Nobel Prize winner is sixty-two, and that, with some exceptions, the prizes generally are awarded for work done in their forties.

Another interesting characteristic of many innovators is what might be called *situational awareness*. Like the aboriginal hunter who recognizes the snap of a twig as dinner-on-the-hoof and responds immediately, the acutely attuned combat Marine whose peripheral vision catches a slight movement to his right that signals trouble, many innovators pick up signs, and perceive a response, that the rest of us will miss. Have you ever been frustrated by not being able to find a cab on a rainy night? Most of us would just curse a little; Travis Kalanick and Garrett Camp came up with the idea we know as Uber.

Rogers Hollingsworth, an economic historian and sociologist, observes that another trait shared by innovators is an appetite for self-learning, reading widely across many fields and disciplines.[2] Innovators are by nature curious about things distant from their immediate zone of interest. Among them is the mechanical engineer who, having forgotten his laptop in the car, picks up *Better Homes and Gardens* in the doctor's waiting room and subconsciously files away tidbits of information and frameworks about kitchen ventilation and garden irrigation. Many self-learners become highly proficient in two or more areas; accomplished avocational musical ability among research physicians is high.[3] Hollingsworth argues that all innovation involves the synthesis of ideas that have not previously been brought together, but that to do so requires knowing something across disparate fields.

In addition to out-and-out knowing more, innovators also are more likely to have honed a skeptical mental predisposition, sometimes referred to as "contrarian thinking."[4] This involves the conscious and subconscious recasting of situations in ways that most people don't see. The historian Herbert Butterfield posits that scientific breakthroughs are the doing of such people who, in his phrase, "see the other end of the stick."[5] Renowned investor Warren Buffett is a contrarian thinker; he ties his wealth to thinking against the wisdom of the crowd, and once attributed his success to being "fearful when others are greedy and to be[ing] greedy only when others are fearful."

When a particular individual is described as having been "born to be an entrepreneur," the commentator usually is trying to describe the innovator's ability to look at the world differently, and to generate something that may have been hiding in plain sight. Any of us might have conceived Uber. All of the pieces existed— underemployed people interested in flexible second jobs to make more money, pervasive cell-phone ownership, and a phone-based payment platform. Why didn't you think of that?

The stories of entrepreneurs that you read here and elsewhere—maybe even on your newsfeed tonight—are linked to new ideas that became the reason for being of a startup company. Is there a bigger picture that explains innovation? That question has been posed for centuries. The answer lies in the creative spirit of humankind, in our absolutely irrepressible organic instinct to invent and improve on our situation. This is the stuff of philosophers, which is available in other books, some of them hundreds of years old. For the moment, when we're concentrating on twenty-first century innovation and progress, consider the following motivations.

## Safety and Security

Even prior to recorded history, the human drive to preserve life and repel predators—the survival instinct—prevailed. We know this not because we've read books or seen the cave paintings, but because we're all here today to read and write about it. As modern individuals and citizens, we continue to seek protection from existential threats. Preparing for war, defensively and offensively, has been the greatest driver of innovation in history. The Defense Advanced Research Projects Agency (DARPA) has cradled innumerable innovations, and the companies that grew from them, to produce widespread benefits that have infused life on earth. An incomplete list includes the Internet (first called the ARPANET), GPS technology that now supports Google and all interactive mapping functions (originally developed for precision bombing), the voice recognition software that powers Siri and Alexa, and three-dimensional mapping that laid the groundwork for 3-D printing (perhaps soon to include printing your replacement liver or kidney).[6]

## Health

Humankind's perpetual and universal quest to delay death, and to reduce disability and infirmity, has spurred every single advance in medicine and nutrition that has made possible our longer and better-quality lives. Hundreds of biotech and agritech firms are started around the world every year, all of which work to convert scientific discoveries into distributable commodities. In the USA, much of this work receives funding from the National Institutes of Health and the Department of Agriculture. This suggests that, as a matter of public policy, we as a society have decided that improving life expectancy and quality is a public good.

### Speed

The bicycle led to the automobile, the airplane, and spaceships, all in our desire to be faster and more efficient in getting from one place to another. Not incidentally, the ability to more quickly communicate with one another was another resulting miracle of faster transit. Recall the couriers of ancient warfare, who ran between battle commanders to report on troop movements and progress, a function that continued largely unchanged through America's Civil War, where written and spoken orders were transmitted via soldiers who raced across battlefields to deliver critical messages. Native Americans and other tribal cultures around the world developed the first form of long-distance visual communication via smoke signals, but radio and field telephones revolutionized the speed of information transfer during the World Wars. We haven't looked back since. Jobs told us that the computer was a means to help the brain work faster. That explains why email was embraced and adopted, at rates of penetration into the population and the frequency of use, faster than any other new invention in human history.

### Leisure and Entertainment

As the developed world moved beyond the full-time job of staying alive, we looked for more and more exciting ways to spend our spare time. One of the first technological advances, which built on the astonishing innovation of photography, was movies. From there, the chain extends to today's virtual reality games, which includes the ability to don goggles and transcend time and space, an experience that has made billionaires of innovators in that realm. On a more conventional, but hardly unprofitable, level, the innovators who bring us entertainment in the modern NFL, NASCAR (the most popular spectator sport in America), and even Cirque du Soleil, are innovators who have reaped enormous rewards. Nearly one in twenty newly created companies every year is devoted to leisure and entertainment products and services.[7]

### Convenience and Comfort

Labor-saving and comfort-enabling devices make up most of this category, which largely operates in tandem with other motivating forces. Dishwashers, garbage disposals, cell phones, and video-streaming services are the simplest modern examples. Consider, however, the big picture of real economic and social change made possible by innovations that we take for granted, such as central air conditioning. Much of the American South, including thriving cities like Dallas, and sites in the world's most arid desserts and swampy lowlands, like Dubai and Singapore, have become thriving economic hubs. This could never have happened without the ability of workers to live comfortably within controlled interior climates, and, also, of course, because we now can artificially maintain climates in which sophisticated electronics can operate.

As long as humankind looks to be safer, live longer, move and communicate more quickly, and has the time to do more than struggle for mere survival for another day, there will be myriad opportunities for innovation. Creating products and services to meet these needs is the business of people who are prepared and motivated to try, and whose inspirations may come from very unexpected quarters. What might motivate you?

---

# A Friend in Trouble

Patrick Ambron is a youthful entrepreneur who is an exception to the more-seasoned innovator rule. Ambron possessed the right combination of entrepreneurial characteristics at the right time, and that right time was when his friend and roommate was in trouble and Ambron wanted to help.

Ambron's roommate, Peter Kistler, was approaching graduation from Syracuse University and applying for jobs. Unfortunately, Kistler shared a name with a sex offender who was serving time in prison. Every Google search highlighted the "Bad Peter," leaving "Good Peter" to struggle with what seemed to be an insurmountable problem. Kistler was at serious risk that all potential employers, most of whom did only cursory preliminary Internet searches on candidates, would continue to confuse him with his incarcerated doppelgänger and summarily dismiss his application. It had already happened several times.

As Ambron worked with Kistler to clear up his identity problem, they discovered that many other people suffered similarly serious predicaments. They also found that there were companies prepared to help, for a steep price. A doctor being badmouthed on the Internet by a disgruntled patient seemed ready to pay handsomely to restore his reputation, and able to pay one company's minimum fee of $25,000 to start the cleanup (with no guarantees of success). Few undergraduates could pony up that kind of money.

Ambron, Kistler, and another SU classmate, Evan McGowan-Watson, reasoned that many college students faced various types of reputation problems that could cost them dearly at the starting gate of their working lives. Perhaps an online profile included pictures of beach party antics? Obscene postings by a rebuffed romantic interest? A misdemeanor citation for standing on a sidewalk with a beer bottle, or a bunch of ignored parking tickets? Most students could never afford to hire one of the established companies to clean up a digital identity.

Ambron was a journalism major, anticipating a career that would begin in a PR firm handling social media for corporate clients. Along the way, he'd studied search-engine logic at Syracuse University's Information School. He knew that it was possible to reshape an individual's reputation by optimizing the number of good stories. The technique involved increasing the frequency of positive Internet references: being named to the Dean's List, winning a marathon, beginning an internship at a nonprofit, or serving as a tutor in a community outreach program, came through loud and clear. Numerous positive references could eventually outrun negative references and Good Peter could overwhelm Bad Peter.

As they worked on solving Kistler's problem, the trio began to see the need for a new company that could provide affordable reputation management. Their entrepreneurial moment came when they saw a unique way to fuse existing software technologies into an actual product that could solve the problem. The differentiating aspect of their solution was that it provided a roadmap to computer savvy students to manage their Internet identities, rather than going to an account manager to perform an expensive one-time repair, which was the business model of the existing reputation management companies. Their student-customers could continuously help to improve and enhance their online profiles.

Ambron and his partners began to develop software that would become their optimization platform, using a subscription model. By eliminating costly personnel who worked on each customer's individual problems, a new company, BrandYourself, structured a business model to provide a product that an undergraduate could afford.

Instead of using expensive television advertising to acquire customers one by one, as did their established competitors, Brand-

Yourself developed a unique approach to attracting clients. The company's founders went directly to universities to sell master-account subscriptions, proposing that the universities provide the company's services free of charge to students preparing to enter the job market. Their first success came at home, when the president of Syracuse University subscribed for every member of the senior class. Shortly thereafter, Johns Hopkins and the University of Rochester signed up, and BrandYourself was off to the races. It wasn't hard for universities to see BrandYourself services not only as effective assistance to their students, but also as a relatively inexpensive gesture of goodwill and support for graduating seniors (and their tuition-paying parents) who would be seeking employment at the end of their college years—who would soon be asked to join the alumni association and support the university's annual fund.

With contract revenue under his belt, Ambron and his partners continued to improve the company's website, making it more friendly for a broader range of customers who likely would be less computer competent than their undergraduate base. BrandYourself decided next to target large corporate accounts, companies that often were dealing with a barrage of nasty customer comments. Over time, universities have been replaced by large companies as the majority of BrandYourself customers, including personal service companies, like money managers, who want to ensure that their employees maintain clean online identities that will encourage customer confidence.

Like many other entrepreneurs who enter a market already occupied by a "first mover," Ambron studied what he saw as his competitors' mistakes. The market leader had raised more than $70 million in venture funding to acquire customers one by one, and their business plan relied on expensive broadcast advertising. Conversely, BrandYourself initially raised less than $1 million from friends and family. Ambron's competitors' higher prices, which reflected their labor-intensive customer management model, resulted in high customer turnover. By selling to large institutions—first universities and then employers—at a substantially lower per-user cost, BrandYourself now retains customers about three times longer than its competitors. The company's data show that many individuals who were BrandYourself customers under a previous employer's umbrella contract continue as individual customers even after they change jobs.

BrandYourself's differentiating value proposition is summed up by Ambron: "It's much cheaper to teach a customer how to prevent a bad reputation from developing in the first place—an offensive approach—than it is to play defense and undo damage after it occurs. Most of our customers have nothing to repair; they use BrandYourself to enhance their online reputations."

In 2016, BrandYourself was invited to appear on *Shark Tank*. After Ambron described the company in the allotted three minutes, the investor panelists seemed excited. Unlike the polite but fruitless reception that most presenters receive, each one of the show's four panelists expressed an interest in investing. Ambron was asked if he would take $2 million for a twenty-five percent share of BrandYourself, meaning that the panelists were judging the total worth of the company to be $8 million, which was much higher than the show's average proposal. Ambron politely countered with $2 million for thirteen percent. All four panelists told him that he was naively overvaluing the company and that no new company could be worth more than $15 million. One judge pushed back hard, saying that $2 million was a generous offer for a quarter of the company and implying that Ambron was making a mistake by being too greedy. Ambron stood his ground. Exasperated, the judge finally asked why he wouldn't take the offer. Ambron's reply was that it would be unfair to his earlier investors, and explained that he had just accepted $3 million from investors who valued BrandYourself at $15 million.

## There's Got to Be a Better Way

Like the rainy night inspiration for Uber, unexpected events and moments of frustration have prompted many innovators to seize upon problems that they thought would be worth solving for themselves and others. When you hand over your credit card in exchange for a pricey YETI cooler, you know that you're paying for unsurpassed performance, durability, and reliability, but you may experience a little twinge as you sign the receipt: "Why didn't I think of this?"

Roy and Ryan Seiders did. The brothers are passionate outdoorsmen who loved to fish in the shallow waters of the Texas Gulf using a skiff. Like most other anglers, they stood atop a cooler to make a long cast. Since the cooler was first introduced in 1954, it has been an essential piece of equipment for fishermen, both keeping beer and soda cold and preserving the day's catch. The first models were made of galvanized steel, but manufacturers shifted to plastic construction in the mid-1960s to meet most customers' preferences for lighter weight and lower cost. But, in 2005, when one more plastic cooler lid collapsed under Ryan, the exasperated brothers decided that someone should make a stronger alternative.

YETI is now the Maserati of coolers. It has engendered stratospheric levels of loyalty among customers, who sometimes are described as cultists. In a market dominated by $30 Igloos, YETI coolers start at about $100 for the smallest models and amp up to the $1400-plus for the gigantic 402-quart Tundra that is advertised as "bear resistant." The brand is defined by its ability to extend

cooling capacity to previously unknown durations, even in swelter-
ing climates, and its rugged strength.

The Seiders revolutionized a market that had not seen a major
product advance in fifty years. Since 2010, YETI has grown more
than 300 percent each year, and is always racing to keep up with
demand. The brothers' aggravation with an inadequate product led
to a "There's got to be a better way" moment, and they then set out
to become cooler experts. YETI's success tells us that they've done
that.

The Seider brothers weren't cooler technology experts, but they
were expert cooler users who decided to solve a problem. At the
other end of the inspiration curve, many other entrepreneurs who
become frustrated with an existing product, process, or service, or
a slow or nonexistent pace of change, come to that moment from
within an industry or market in which they have had long and deep
experience, and which may be the very industry that is producing
the source of their frustration.

Leo Goodwin took his first job with the United Services Automobile Association insurance company, now universally known as
USAA, in San Diego. USAA had been created in 1922 to sell auto
insurance to active duty military personnel, who had difficulty purchasing insurance from other carriers because they were not per-
manent residents of the states in which they were stationed.

As Goodwin turned fifty, he recognized that he wouldn't be
promoted further in a company that was headed by retired military officers, so he decided to start his own company, based on
the knowledge and experience that he had gained. A seasoned underwriter, Goodwin concluded that government employees were
better insurance risks than members of the military, and that he
could reduce the cost of car insurance for public workers by selling directly, without agents. In 1936, when the country was still in

the throes of the Depression, Goodwin moved to Washington and founded the Government Employees Insurance Company. What we now know as GEICO grew quickly. The company went public in 1948. It now has more than fourteen million customers, both within and without government service, and offers a wide range of insurance products.[8]

Another story of deep industry experience begetting a new business comes in the person of Wally Blume, who spent his first lifetime managing dairy products for Kroger, the national grocery chain. After retiring Blume leveraged his knowledge into Denali Flavors, the home of Moose Tracks ice cream, but he didn't stop there. His Kroger experience had taught him the critical importance of scale—he did not want just to become another artisanal ice cream brand—and, in 2006, Denali Ingredients was created to manufacture a broad range of ice-cream flavoring products for ice-cream makers all over the country.

Morris Chang's story makes the case for the manner in which extensive tech industry experience, coupled with a predisposition to see where a breakthrough startup might fill an undetected market need, can be a route to innovation. Chang's first job was working at Texas Instruments with Jack Kilby, the Nobel Prize–winning physicist who had invented the integrated circuit. The company made the first pocket calculators, one of the first consumer applications of small-scale computing capacity. The device relied on a circuit board, an array of transistors soldered together on a tiny piece of plastic, etched, and coated with sophisticated materials that controlled the flow of tiny electrical charges. To make chips, Texas Instruments had to build a dedicated fabrication facility that cost hundreds of millions of dollars.

Kilby's innovation had kicked off a new profession of electrical designers that created an enormous demand for customized circuit boards. The technology that had enabled TI's remarkable success now presented a problem. TI could expand and become the world's largest supplier of chips, but the cost of meeting this demand was overwhelming and the company couldn't keep up with the demand for customized chips.

Chang saw that the company's limitations were related to its not being able to retool production facilities fast enough. He returned home and started Taiwan Semiconductor Manufacturing Company. There, he devised a way to quickly reengineer the process of making chips, allowing him to supply the burgeoning global demand. His silicon foundry helped fuel a tidal wave of innovation. Suddenly, consumer products were becoming "smart." Televisions and washing machines were programmable; mechanical control systems in cars were replaced by computers that improved mileage and greatly reduced the cost of repairs; and airplane-control systems were revamped, ushering in the age of the "glass cockpit" and safer flying. Thanks in part to Chang, every home with children suddenly had a box stuffed with circuitry connected to its televisions. The era of gaming, replete with joysticks, had begun.

## Birthing a Birthing Business

Like the founders of BrandYourself, Amy Upchurch had never worked in a company. Her personal experiences, her drive to help others in like circumstances, and her tenacity, made her into an entrepreneur.

When Upchurch was pregnant with her first child, she suffered debilitating bouts of morning sickness, so serious that she was hospitalized on and off throughout. The same severe problems plagued her second and third pregnancies. As the wife of a Marine officer, she had lived in different places for each pregnancy, and nearly a dozen doctors had attempted to help her with various drugs and diet regimens. Nothing had worked. When Upchurch became pregnant with her fourth child, she vowed that this time would be different; she would figure out how to avoid the pain and constant nausea with which she'd lived three times before. With three young children and an often-absent husband, she simply couldn't be sick all the time.

Upchurch had learned that morning sickness most often is caused by a stomach bacteria, *Helicobacter pylori*, that can be killed with antibiotics. *H. pylori* resides in about half the human population, and is now known to be the principal cause of stomach ulcers. In some women, their normal colony of *H. pylori* explodes with the hormonal changes of pregnancy, resulting in severe nausea. In about half of these women, antibiotics solve the problem. In the other half, including Upchurch, the antibiotic therapy had no effect.

As she began to research the medical aspects of morning sickness, and to read thousands of blog entries by pregnant women who shared her condition, Upchurch began to think that a multimodal approach, using diet supplements, might be the answer. It was certainly worth a try. After a lot of study and self-experimentation, her combination of probiotics, herbal teas, and cocolaurin, a natural alkaloid extract of coconut that had been shown to inhibit *H. pylori*, worked. Her uncomplicated fourth pregnancy produced a beautiful baby boy.

Upchurch wanted to help other women by sharing what she'd learned. At first, she considered starting a blog about her experience. She finally decided that others would take the findings of her research, and her recommendations as to what had worked for her, much more seriously—that she could be of more real help to others—if she provided products that expectant mothers could purchase and use. Within a few months of delivering her son, Upchurch was thinking like an entrepreneur. In the summer of 2014, she incorporated Pink Stork to be a one-stop source for products to help with morning sickness.

Before going to market, Upchurch tested and evaluated a wide range of more refined solutions than she had initially had the time to do for herself. She settled on a topical magnesium spray to control nausea, a probiotic to improve the functioning of the immune system and to provide the extra nutrients needed in pregnancy, then the cocolaurin tablets to keep the *H. pylori* at bay. She located a nutraceutical manufacturer to compound her products. Upchurch then worked on a branding strategy that included testing multiple images for the company, and for each product. Finally, she decided that she had to sell directly through the Internet.

Twelve months after Upchurch had the idea for Pink Stork, she was ready to launch. She went live with a website but no advertising budget, relying on nothing but tweets and likes on social media. Sales were slow at first but the trajectory was positive; twelve months later, sales were doubling each month, and Pink Stork was making money. Upchurch moved her business out of her kitchen and hired part-time helpers to fill orders. At fifteen months, Pink Stork sales revenues permitted her to pay back her investor; meaning herself, as she and her husband had raided their savings to start the company. In the parlance of investors, Pink Stork was cash-flow positive; revenues were exceeding expenses. Now, Upchurch has her products in large national retailers including Walmart and Target.

Upchurch's story is one of circumstance. She had the miserable personal experiences of difficult pregnancies; as she learned from her research, her problems were not unique. She had a predisposition to help others with her newfound information. After all, she'd had a multitude of caring health professionals striving to assist, but to no avail. What about that sick-as-a-dog pregnant woman who

---

thought that there was no hope? The need for Pink Stork's products came upon Upchurch without calculus or notice; if anything, she was a reluctant entrepreneur. Upchurch had a busy and wonderful life underway as a military wife and mother of four. She had majored in journalism, not biology. To start a business required her to master not only product content but also supply chain management, website design, and Internet sales. Lucky for Upchurch that she didn't stop to write a business plan.

## Innovating with Knowledge Acquired Along the Way

A pair of entrepreneurs whom I met several years ago now operate a company that has moved well beyond the startup stage. Their story is as unlikely as any of you can imagine; it personifies the combination of circumstance combined with just enough background knowledge, and some significant daring. Sheex, the performance-bedding manufacturer now found in many major retail outlets, offers bed sheets and sleepwear that "phase adjust" to wick moisture away from a sleeper's skin and accommodate changing body temperatures throughout the night, both retaining heat when the sleeper's body temp drops, and releasing it when the body warms. All this, and it's soft to the touch, which was a threshold requirement in the founders' development process.

I met Michelle Brooke-Marciniak and Susan Walvius in 2010, when a mutual friend asked if I would talk with them about their business concept. Both were well known in the world of women's basketball, Brooke-Marciniak having played on the University of Tennessee team that won the Final Four in 1996, when she was named MVP, and Walvius as one of the best-known coaches in the country.

One afternoon, when coaching together at the University of South Carolina, Brooke-Marciniak casually remarked that today's high-tech fabrics had made uniforms—and playing—much more comfortable than the poly-based mesh that they'd worn when they'd been on the court. Walvius agreed, observing that it was too bad that people couldn't sleep on the same kind of performance fabrics. Instead of Walvius' observation being just a part of casual courtside banter, Brooke-Marciniak and Walvius followed up. Should someone try to make sheets out of similar material? Should they be the ones to try? They soon found themselves in the university's chemistry department, where a professor agreed to help.

The two didn't know it at the time, but they were kicking off a process of materials engineering that produced a new fabric and a new product. They raised money from friends and family and contracted with a mill in China to make samples of their new fabric. This was no easy task for novices to the notoriously complex fabric production business. A local seamstress made prototypes of several dozen sheets that they asked friends to try. The response was more than enthusiastic; everyone wanted to buy them. With these findings, their entrepreneurial decision point was at hand.

Both Brooke-Marciniak and Walvius loved their coaching jobs. Basketball had been their recreation and their professions. They knew nothing about business, were in midcareer, and had secure employment. The idea of starting a business that would require them to manage manufacturing, supply chains, and sales through retail channels was daunting. They were certain, however, that people would want what they had to offer. When, early on in their journey, I asked them to describe the future of Sheex, their answer reflected the determination of championship competitors and passionate entrepreneurs: "In ten years, we want to see a Sheex ad during the Super Bowl."

Both knew that their new game was to make a market for their innovative sheets, and both understood that sales and sales alone would determine if Sheex had a future. They caught a huge break when a friend of a friend arranged an introduction to Bed Bath & Beyond. The chain, one of the nation's largest home-goods outlets, agreed to place their sheets in a few test-market stores. Would their sheets be worth BB&B's shelf space, every retailer's most valuable asset? The response was overwhelming and, in only a few months, Sheex was in every BB&B store. Today, Sheex bedding and sleepwear also is sold in specialized athletic retailers, like Dick's Sporting Goods, and several large retailers like Target and Walmart. Seven years after Sheex launched, sales were up one-hundred percent over the previous year.

When I asked how their lives as players and coaches had prepared them for the competition of business, Walvius offered an interesting insight. "Running Sheex is nothing like a basketball game. In business, the court is always changing dimensions; one corner is higher now and lower a minute later. There is a hole in the middle of the floor, there are three hoops one minute and five the next. Each player on the other team is wearing a different uniform, the ball is constantly changing size, there is no clock, and the refs are blind." Basketball, she continued, was easy by comparison; "You practiced, played, and either won or lost." As an entrepreneur, she said, the game just keeps going with no ending buzzer. "There's no just getting through forty minutes." Success requires nonstop, persistent innovations, and discipline, measured in years.

## Please Let Me Know if There's Anything I Can Do to Help

Who hasn't said these words to an ill or injured family member or friend, or to an exhausted caregiver? The words feel hollow when we speak or write them, and we are left with the option of sending flowers or some silly token to try to express our concern, or turning into a nag who repeatedly calls to ask the same question. When you live within reasonable driving distance from your loved one in need, providing support by delivering lasagna or taking a carpool shift can be easy, but what if you don't? Susan Bratton thought about this conundrum in a new way.

Bratton grew up in rural Colorado, studied political science at Duke, and earned her MBA at the University of Virginia. For twenty years, Bratton worked in New York City as an investment banker specializing in health care; she was involved in financing major corporate acquisitions and mergers involving drug companies, hospital systems, HMOs, and nursing homes. Bratton also assisted many fledgling biotech firms in obtaining initial financing and saw many of them through their public offering. She was fascinated by the continuously changing intersection of medicine and business and was regarded as one of the best bankers in the field.

In 2012, Bratton's close friend was diagnosed with brain cancer. Throughout her friend's long illness, Bratton was surprised at how little attention the medical team paid to his nutrition: What could make him feel better, what would not conflict or interfere with the efficacy of medications, what would simply comfort him? She researched the issue and discovered that very little attention had been devoted to individualized nutritional support for people fighting certain diseases. Meals to Heal was born. As Bratton told me, "I decided that something had to be done, and if I didn't take up the challenge, no one else would."

Bratton invested most of her personal savings and, using just a few slides to demonstrate her idea, was able to persuade several investors to help fund her startup. Her initial marketing strategy was to convince local New York City hospital nutrition counselors to suggest Meals to Heal to international patients who were temporarily residing in the city while receiving outpatient cancer treatments. Bratton found a commercial kitchen in Los Angeles that would prepare customized meals consistent with the dietary protocols recommended for each patient. The meals were individually prepared, frozen, and shipped to the hotels or apartments where the patients were staying. A few minutes in the microwave yielded a hot and nutritious meal.

Although Bratton received an enthusiastic reception from a cadre of wealthy international patients, scaling a customer base proved very difficult. Acquiring each customer required multiple conversations with physicians or nutritionists to persuade them to recommend the company's product. Even so, word of mouth spread the company's mission in the hospital-nutrition community, and Bratton began to hear from nutritionists across the country asking how their patients could access the service. Still, the volume of business wasn't enough to sustain the company, and Bratton concluded that her sales approach and supply chain would have to change.

Bratton did what many entrepreneurs find very hard to do: She threw her business model overboard and started again. Because she had seen other companies take similarly radical steps as a banker, she knew that sometimes it was necessary to reshape a business from the ground up in order to survive. As a part of her reboot, Bratton jettisoned the name Meals to Heal, and gave her company a new brand, Savor Health.

Harkening back to the roots of her entrepreneurial inspiration—wanting to help her friend, but not knowing what to do—Bratton wondered if supportive family and friends were the new customers that her company needed to most effectively deliver her service. She experimented with using the Internet to sell gift cards for specially formulated meals that could be purchased and sent as expressions of caring and love. The market responded almost immediately. Now, Bratton can sell a gift card to a customer in Houston who wants to do something meaningful for a sick friend in Seattle. Thanks to the new phenomenon of last-mile delivery, something that didn't exist when Bratton founded her company, Savor Health can get meals to homes all over the country, often within a matter of hours.

As a banker, Bratton had a ringside seat as failing companies tried to remake their businesses. She was like a general who had studied historic battles; she knew that every startup faces an unpredictable market and that, if her objective was to be achieved, a new strategy was needed. Bratton also knew that, had she solicited investors based on a detailed written plan, she might have found those funders reluctant to endorse such a profound shift in her target market, sales strategy, and production methods. Now on a new path, Bratton is pioneering a new business by the marriage of the old and the new: The desire to be of true assistance to those in need is as old as human civilization. Savor Health is seeking to help by offering products that emphasize the new and important role of nutrition in patient recovery and comfort and, using new superfast delivery capacities, new food preparation, and freezing techniques, with the new capacity to reach customers far and wide via Internet marketing and sales.

What inspires or motivates anyone to become an entrepreneur? The stories here suggest two ingredients go into the decision to start a company. Someone sees herself filling a need for others with a new product or service. Making something new to which the market responds, being the first to do so, entering into an unknown world by starting a company that could fail or make her wealthy, all suggest challenges that excite every entrepreneur. All these entrepreneurs were at moments in their careers at which they could consider new life plans and take on the challenges of starting companies. All implicitly weighed their circumstances, and the possibilities that awaited them if they let the entrepreneurial moment pass. Some had secure employment, mortgages, family obligations, or pending job offers. While such considerations hold others back, entrepreneurs choose the path of adventure. They set out to make *the new*, and in the process to make a different life for themselves. Some, as we will see shortly, can't help themselves.

# CHAPTER 5

# Can You Survive the Entrepreneur's Curse?

When successful entrepreneurs reminisce, many wryly reflect that the good old days were anything but, and that their successes were anything but likely. Most startups, even those that are built on great ideas and successful execution, take a long time to bloom. The "entrepreneur's curse" is being possessed with a consuming focus—sometimes described as an obsession—on their innovation, while at the same time living with uncertainty, doubt, and even fear during an indeterminate period, waiting to see if their vision is something that the market will value.

James Dyson grew up in rural England. His father taught Latin and Greek in a private boys school, and his family expected Dyson to follow in that tradition, to go to university and take a degree in classics. How did Dyson end up designing a revolutionary vacuum cleaner and founding a company that has an unparalleled reputation for engineering and design innovation?

It started with a revolt against his family's plan for his career. At nineteen, Dyson enrolled in art school in London. Through a chance meeting, he was hired by an engineer, Jeremy Fry, who was devising a new utility boat that he came to call the Sea Truck. Dyson became fascinated with the intersection of design and engineering and helped as Fry started his new company, successfully selling his Sea Trucks as workboats and military landing craft.

Perhaps it was because Dyson had participated in a union of design and engineering that he noticed how one of our most common and necessary home appliances worked so badly. One day, while "hoovering," he noticed that his machine continuously lost more and more suction power as its bag filled. He borrowed a few friends' vacuum cleaners and found that the problem was endemic. Seeking the source of the design flaw, he examined the paper bags used to collect dirt and realized that the pores that allowed air to pass through while capturing debris were clogging up quickly with fine particles.

How could it be, he wondered, that the vacuum cleaner, a household appliance that had become a necessity in the developed world and had a phenomenal market penetration, could perform so badly? Why hadn't someone made a better machine? After a little study, Dyson came upon the obvious: Every machine periodically required replacement bags. The vacuum industry's business model was akin to Gillette's: Make the razor to sell the blades. Dyson decided that he could make a better machine, whose improved suction would clean better and would eliminate the continually recurring expense of bag replacement.

Dyson's interest in making a new kind of vacuum cleaner grew serious. For the next decade, he devoted himself to his vacuum cleaner project, exhausting his savings and relying on his wife's income as an art teacher to support their family of five. Much like Thomas Edison and his light bulb, Dyson built over five thousand prototypes of vacuum cleaners, observing how each could be improved. Slowly, his experiments began to point to a design that required sucking air into the vacuum at over nine hundred miles per hour, then separating the airstream into two opposing directions. The idea was prompted by seeing how sawmills gathered up sawdust as they cut lumber. The gap of calm air in between the facing airstreams let the dirt carried by each fall into a bagless chamber. Dyson was so proud of his "dual cyclonic" innovation that he decided to make the machine mostly of clear plastic, so that users could have the satisfaction of seeing dirt accumulate in the chamber as they cleaned their floors.

In 1983, when Dyson was satisfied with his design, he approached several manufacturers with the certain belief that they would license his idea. What he hadn't realized was the depth of the industry's commitment to its existing business model; the manufacturers had no interest in disrupting their replacement paper-bag business, much less in retooling to a completely new manufacturing process. Every U.S. and British manufacturer rejected his proposals.

Eventually, a Japanese company decided to produce his machine, and the bagless cleaner met with great success. Next, a Canadian company licensed his design; its dual cyclonic models created skyrocketing demand. Sales were so strong that Dyson found himself having to vigorously defend his patents against some of the same American and British companies that previously had shown him the door.

In 1993, using profits from his global licensing agreements, Dyson founded his own manufacturing and development company. Its objective was to supply his improved vacuum design to both the British and American markets. He was forty-six years old, and vacuum cleaners had been his life for nearly twenty years.

---

Along the path to vacuum cleaner perfection, however, Dyson had developed increasing confidence in his abilities to meld the insights of design and engineering, and he was eager to apply those ideas to other problems. He had built his company, and its facilities, as creative hybrids, a combination of design studio and factory, and he was determined to continue on that path.

In his new environment, Dyson could spend time on innovative designs and test their feasibility as production models at the same time. He began to work on other consumer needs. Soon, in addition to manufacturing new generations of vacuums, each more efficient than the last, Dyson was making other products that many of us encounter every day, including cyclonic hand dryers, and his noise-free, bladeless fan, the Air Multiplier. His improved and beautiful designs for other products, including washing machines and water heaters, continue to emerge.

## Reimagining Skis

Dyson is an innovator-entrepreneur, one of a relatively small group who have both invented new products and then started and managed successful manufacturing companies. While many innovator-entrepreneurs combine existing state-of-the-art technologies and apply them to new, unforeseen uses to meet human needs, Dyson went full-bore at a fundamental reinvention of aging, inadequate technology.

Howard Head was a like spirit. In 1947, when Head was working as an aircraft engineer in Baltimore, he spent a week's vacation taking skiing lessons in Mt. Mansfield in Vermont, home to one of the nation's first ski schools. Head was not a born athlete. He was six feet four, very thin, and awkward. On skis, a friend once observed, "Howard looked like a skinny gorilla whose knees wouldn't bend."

Head was very frustrated after his first few lessons. His heavy skis, which were made from solid wood—much as they had been for five thousand years—refused to go where he directed. He badly wanted to be able to ski like his instructors, effortlessly slaloming down the slopes and experiencing an exhilaration that Head could practically taste. On his train back home, Head had a brainstorm. Maybe he could ski better if his skis were more user friendly—if they somehow worked for him, not against him.

Perhaps this insight derived from his day job as an aeronautical engineer, where he engaged in a continual process of making airplanes fly faster while, at the same time, being more responsive to the pilot. Maybe if skis were constructed of something lighter than hickory, then the preferred wood, they'd be easier to steer and maybe even faster. Head told me that he remembered doodling on a napkin in the bar car, drawing cross sections of a new ski made from aircraft aluminum and plastic, and said that he'd talked about his idea with a soldier who sat across the table. The soldier urged Head to give it a try: "After designing bombers, making better skis should be a cinch."

Back in Baltimore at the Glenn L. Martin Aircraft Company, Head began to gather bits of scrap materials. At night and on weekends, he began to experiment. Because skis were so long, he had to rent several old adjoining garages in the alley behind his apartment. That dim and unheated site was the workshop from which the modern snow ski would emerge. But, like Dyson's ingenious vacuum cleaner, Head's improvement would take some time.

As a first try, Head used shoemaker's glue to sandwich a plastic honeycomb between two pieces of aluminum, which he then covered with an outer sheet of plastic. To permanently bond the layers together, he inserted the skis into a rubber bag that served as a vacuum chamber to eliminate bubbles in the glue. Then, to make his prototypes more flexible, he dipped them in boiling crankcase oil. The process was smelly, dangerous, and highly toxic.

In the meantime, Head's finances were straining under the cost of tools, materials, and rent. So, like Ewing Kauffman, Head hustled up card games when he needed cash. After eleven months of bluffing at poker and tinkering in his workshop, Head thought that he was ready to unveil the future of skiing. He returned to Mt. Mansfield. One cold morning, he invited the instructors to meet in the ski school's lodge, where Head showed them the first five pairs of aluminum-plastic skis that had ever been made.

One of the instructors gave the first of the shiny skis a vigorous shake. It came apart in his hands. A second instructor pushed the top of another ski into the floor, where it promptly disintegrated. The instructors took turns flexing more skis, and the laminated layers came apart on every one. With only one pair left, Head asked the instructors to watch him demonstrate how they worked on snow. As they gathered at the top of the bunny slope, Head slowly skied down the gentle hill. His skis came apart beneath his boots, leaving him in a tangled heap of twisted metal and broken plastic.

Despite this discouraging debut, Head remained determined to make better skis. This became even more daunting when he became aware that he had competition, not an uncommon experience for innovator–entrepreneurs. A group of engineers from another aircraft company had begun to market an all-aluminum ski; the next winter, they manufactured several thousand pairs. Their product was heavy, however, and the metal surface could not hold wax. Worse, when a skier hit an ice patch the skis were impossible to control, making a hideous screeching noise and dumping the wearer into a snow bank. Head remained optimistic. He was sure that his vision of an aluminum and plastic ski held promise.

The quest for better skis had taken over Head's life. After two years of off-hours moonlighting and very little sleep, he quit his day job. Without regular employment, and having run out of suckers to outplay at the card table, he moved to a dingy basement apartment. On cold days he went without heat, wearing his father's old overcoat. He borrowed money to eat and buy materials, and could no longer afford to pay the two after-hours aircraft mechanics who were assisting him. Fortunately, they believed in Head's dream and kept on working, recording their hours on the wall of the workshop so that, if he was ever successful, he could pay them. (Which he did, and then some.)

Head tried different combinations of plastic, metal, and plywood to create the combination of strength and flexibility that he needed. He experimented with various plastics for the ski's bottom to prevent icing. He scraped together enough money to buy three used restaurant ovens and welded them together, experimenting with laminating plastic and metal together with heat to make the skis more durable. Head returned to Mt. Mansfield again and again, where the group of patient, but now intrigued, instructors continued to test his evolving prototypes. They may have found Head a bit ridiculous at first, but, over time, they came to appreciate his indomitable creative spirit and his devotion to their sport.

By 1951, Head had succeeded in making a notably better ski. "Head Standards" were significantly lighter than wooden skis, and turned with half the effort. That year, he sold 1,100 pairs out of the back of his station wagon, setting up in parking lots at the bottom of ski slopes, and wearing a quirky raccoon coat to attract attention. Sales continued to grow, but Head also kept innovating; he added neoprene between the metal layers to reduce the "chatter" as his skis rode over bumps. While his skis were generally well received, they were not dominating the sport as Head knew that they should.

In a moment of marketing inspiration, Head convinced a talented young French Alpine racer to try his skis. In the 1968 Winter

Olympics, Jean-Claude Killy was on Head skis when he won gold medals in all three Alpine events. Head ski sales exploded. The next year, more than eighty percent of ski instructors, and a third of competitors in top international races, were on Heads. Two years later, fifty percent of American skiers bought Head's skis, and the company sold 400,000 pairs across seventeen countries. In 1970, at the age of fifty-four and twenty-three years after his first humiliation at Mt. Mansfield, Head sold his company to AMF and retired.

## Staying in the Game

With time on his hands, money in the bank, and a yet unfulfilled desire to be good at the sports he enjoyed, Head built a tennis court at his home and hired a pro. He was a terrible player. His coach told Head that he'd quit if Head didn't improve, so Head bought one of the first machines that shot balls across the net and doggedly practiced his stroke technique.

Not surprisingly, Head was not very pleased with how the ball machine worked. He couldn't resist the urge to tinker with it, and was spending more time improving the machine than practicing tennis. Once he had reengineered the machine, he visited its tiny manufacturer, Prince and, shortly thereafter, bought a controlling interest in the company. Head was back in the business of improving sports equipment.

Playing better tennis was now something of a business imperative for him, but he now had less time to practice than ever. Predictably, Head began to wonder if he could improve his game if his racquet were better.

Head had a complete machine shop in his house where he made a few racquets of aluminum. He noticed, like their traditional wood counterparts, they twisted when hitting the ball, which he thought might be part of his problem in getting the most from his swing. To correct for unwanted torque, he reinforced the racquet's shaft and made some parts of the rim thicker than others. That didn't help. After six months of experimentation, Head explained, the answer came to him when he was relaxing in an easy chair and listening to Bach: Instead of trying to redistribute the racquet's weight, he needed to make its face bigger and wider.

Head then discovered something that he found astonishing. In the hyperconservative world of tennis, governed by hundreds of rules promulgated by the U.S. Lawn Tennis Association (as it was then named) that covered everything from the color of clothing on the court to what to do if a ball fell out of your pocket, a racquet was defined simply as "an implement used to strike the ball." Former Wimbledon champion Bobby Riggs had once won a match using a broom. Realizing that an oversized racquet face and frame could be his answer, Head made a few. He hired Kenneth Wright, an engineer at Princeton, to help him dissect the aerodynamics of a tennis racquet. Head and Wright locked experimental racquets into vises and shot tennis balls at them, recording the strike using time-lapse photography. They studied the speed at which balls bounced off various racquets from every area of its face. They were searching for the precise location of the "sweet spot," the place on the racquet's face that repelled the ball at the fastest speed.

Conventional wisdom had always located the sweet spot in the center of the racquet face, but Head and Wright found that it actually was much closer to the racquet's shaft. By designing a racquet with a larger head, they could move the sweet spot to the center, making it easier for players to hit stronger serves and volleys. Even more important, they discovered that the sweet spot on the new, larger, graphite-plastic racquet also was larger—about four times its size on a traditional racquet. These discoveries allowed Head to design a bigger racquet that wouldn't torque and increased a player's odds of hitting a strong, clean shot.

The result looked like a "cross between a cruise missile and an endangered balloon fish."[1] Traditionalists dismissed it as a gimmick, but Head knew exactly what to do: He made sure that a number of tennis professionals had the chance to try a Prince Oversize. He persuaded Don Candy, the pro at his country club in Baltimore, to get a few of his students to play with his new racquet. Candy gave a Prince Oversize to fourteen-year-old Pam Shriver. The big racquet suited her powerful serve-and-volley game. It also fit her personality; Shriver didn't mind the snickering from other players when she stepped onto the court with her peculiar weapon. In 1978, at just sixteen, she took the U.S. Open by storm, brushing aside top seed Martina Navratilova in the semi-finals. Although she was narrowly defeated by Chris Evert in the finals, Shriver's unusual racquet quickly started to appear on courts across the country. The large "P" stenciled across the racquet face left no doubt about its maker. Twelve years after Head had bought a tennis-ball machine, he retired for a second time when he sold Prince.

## What Is "Entrepreneur's Time"?

Head was the first entrepreneur whom I knew well. When our family, with a new baby, moved into our house, I learned that the retired guy down the street was the man who had revolutionized skiing *and* tennis. We lived on a nearly blind curve and quickly learned that it was Head's habit to blow his car's horn in a continuous blast as he drove through the curve. After about the tenth time that Head's horn had awakened our hard-to-get-to-sleep son, I stepped out into the street when I spotted him coming and put up my hand. He stopped, and I said, "Hi, I know that you're Howard Head and that you're an engineer. You of all people should know that sound doesn't travel around a curve." After a moment's pause,

Head burst into laughter. We were invited to dinner soon thereafter, and became good friends.

Tall and unassuming, Head was textbook geeky and, at first, a bit shy. Like many other innovators of great talent and drive, he was quick to say that he wasn't anyone special, that he had been lucky enough to stumble onto his life's purpose. I was in the midst of building my first company and spent as much time talking with Head as I could. My biggest question to him, which is the same one that I ask every entrepreneur today, was, "How did you decide to start your business?" Head's answer was particularly thoughtful. In his case, Head said, he had no choice. He saw himself as cursed by never being able to look at or use an object without seeing that it needed to be better. As the story of his reengineering of the Prince ball machine shows, he just couldn't keep himself from trying to improve things.

Upon reflection, Head mused that, when a personality like his starts to work on a new product, he doesn't really know how long it might take to get to the finish line. That type of person, Head observed, slips into "entrepreneur's time," a corollary of the entrepreneur's curse. The innovator walls off the pressure of time, knowing that no matter how long it may take, he wants to get to a new product that is as close to perfection as he can make it.

Head made a second observation, one relating to the relationship of time and innovation. He said that it takes about twice as long for a new product to become accepted by the market as it takes to invent it. It took more than ten years after Head had developed a better ski before skiers understood what he'd accomplished, and slightly less for his Prince tennis racquet to upset the tennis world.

Were Head alive now, I wonder if his thesis would have changed: With today's lightning-fast communications and direct-to-consumer marketing possibilities via the Internet, perhaps that 2:1 ratio no longer pertains. Has the cycle shortened? Notwithstanding the speed of market adoption of new products, perhaps Head's basic thesis still holds: All innovation results from taking a new idea to market, absorbing customer feedback to improve its design, and repeating or iterating the process until the market is receptive.[2] Both Head and Dyson sought to replace products that no one thought needed improving. Their self-certain visions that the world needed better vacuum cleaners, skis, and tennis racquets, but didn't know it, brings to mind Henry Ford's observation that, if asked what they wanted, his potential customers would have answered, "faster horses." Steve Jobs thought the same way when he said, "Customers don't know what they want until we've shown them."

## Reinventing a Market and Growing Faster Than Apple

Just as Paul Stebbins graduated from college in 1979, the economy tanked. His job prospects were "limited, bordering on none," so he returned home to Connecticut. Steve, the Stebbins family's next-door neighbor, had been asked by a cousin in Greece to buy fuel for his only freighter, a vessel that he was about to send to New York for the first time with a cargo of general merchandise from Europe. The ship needed to be refueled so that it could return home, and Steve's cousin needed someone in America to purchase fuel oil. Steve's only qualification to help was that he was family, that is, deemed trustworthy, and that he spoke Greek. Holding down his regular job by day, Steve took a crash course on the phone with his Greek cousin on how to buy fuel every night for weeks. Steve needed help.

He hired Stebbins part time to run back and forth to New York with piles of documents that were a part of buying fuel oil, and told Stebbins to keep his eyes and ears open and to learn as much as he could. Delivering documents, Stebbins' job took him down into the engine rooms of freighters, to pier-side oil terminals, to the wire rooms of international banks, and sometimes into fancy law offices in Manhattan. Stebbins became intrigued with what he learned. At night, he would return to Connecticut and report to Steve, and they began to figure out how oil was being bought and sold. Stebbins had majored in international affairs in college; what he was observing seemed to him to be the tangible, real-time commerce that his textbooks had described.

Infected with the excitement of the business, Stebbins landed a full-time job at a New York brokerage firm, where he traded fuel oil. He was good at spot transactions, which provided him with a handsome income for a guy in his twenties. But he was equally interested in the larger dynamics of international oil markets. As he recalls, "I could tell something bigger was going on. Gradually, the number of companies selling oil in the world market was growing. More oil was being produced by smaller firms that no one had ever heard of, who were operating in remote corners of the globe. The market for fuel oil was becoming chaotic. The old forces that made for stability in oil prices were slowly eroding."

At the same time that Stebbins entered the brokerage business, so had Michael Kasbar. His path to trading oil was as serendipitous as Stebbins. When Kasbar's mother vetoed his taking a job as an assistant bread baker, telling him that she expected more of her college-educated son, he restarted his job search. One day, when he was reading a newspaper story that projected that the oil industry would lead the economy out of recession, Kasbar decided where to look. Using the Manhattan Yellow Pages, he started calling companies that identified themselves as being in the oil business. Eventually, he got a job at a marine-fuel brokerage firm.

Kasbar and Stebbins met by chance about five years after each had started trading oil. Comparing notes, they agreed that the standard sources for ships' fuel, major oil companies like Exxon and Shell, appeared to be devoting more and more of their attentions to exploration, drilling, and refining higher-priced fuels. As a result, new and untested suppliers of small lots were coming into the market, and the supply of consistently reliable fuel oil was dwindling. Without predictable sources, traders had to pull oil from several, often unknown, refiners to assemble complete orders.

The specter of disaster loomed over these patchwork deals. Once bunker oil from a variety of different refineries was mixed and pumped on board, there was no tracing the source of any bad oil. That mattered a lot. The risk was that a ship would be stuck at sea because its fuel was adulterated with poorly refined product. The expense and financial consequence of having to rescue a disabled freighter on the high seas was enormous; empty ships had to be dispatched to take on stranded cargo, ocean-going tugs were needed to pull the disabled ship to port, late delivery of cargo could result in huge penalties to the shipping companies, and, worst of all, an affected ship usually had to go to dry dock to be refurbished with new engines, a big-ticket process that could take months. Without the ability to trace fuel to its source, there was no legal recourse for the significant damages. The risk of tyro suppliers was spinning out of control.

After long conversations with potential customers and suppliers, Kasbar and Stebbins left their jobs to found Trans-Tec Services, a marine-fuel brokerage, in 1985. They convinced a Greek shipping mogul (not Steve's cousin) to bankroll their startup. With a good balance sheet, they were able to begin buying futures contracts from dependable sources. Big shipping companies became Trans-Tec's customers because they needed assurance as to the quality, quantity, and reliability of their fuel. Because they were buying oil in such large quantities, Kasbar and Stebbins acquired more knowledge about the direction of the global oil market than most other buyers and sellers, allowing them to profitably buy and sell futures contracts.

As Trans-Tec grew and its market power increased, the company established and enforced trading and testing standards to ensure the quality of the oil that refiners supplied. The company also developed important innovations, including better ways for ships to rendezvous and refuel in midocean. Trans-Tec was on its way to becoming the world's biggest marine fuel and service provider.

For some time, Kasbar and Stebbins had been considering expansion into the aviation market, but they needed more resources. After identifying a larger company, IRC, that had complementary assets, they entered into a sale transaction that eventually put them in charge of the larger company. Slowly, they began to remodel their new parent into a company that could capture the exponential growth that Kasbar and Stebbins had envisioned—becoming the largest independent global supplier of marine *and* jet fuel, now known as World Fuel Services.

Their strategy worked. Supplying airlines with jet fuel turned out to be an even bigger market than supplying ocean-going vessels. Moving into aviation allowed their global company to develop the world's most exclusive business credit card to serve the private aircraft industry, and to begin to supply logistics services, including ground transport. Thirty-three years after two young guys started Trans-Tec, World Fuel Services customers include entire navies, huge shipping and cruise ship lines, many of the world's largest air carriers, and trucking companies worldwide. The company does business in two hundred countries and employs four thousand people. Its annual revenues exceed $40 billion, more than many better-known companies on the *Fortune 100* list. For the ten year period from 2003 to 2013, World Fuel Services' growth outpaced even Apple, providing the highest return to its investors of any publicly traded stock.

Kasbar and Stebbins are much like Dyson and Head. They saw a way to solve a problem that others had yet to recognize, much less act upon. By envisioning a way to enter the global-supply chain for fuel, then leveraging their knowledge and experience, they became a global force.

## Startups as Innovation Platforms

Stebbins told me that the success of Trans-Tec, and eventually World Fuel Services, was related to how he and Kasbar saw themselves as outsiders in the world of fuel brokerage. Their vision of controlling oil quality from the refinery to its delivery to a customer's vessel was a new approach to their business. They heard, "That can't be done," time and time again from old hands in the business who knew much more than they did, yet they remained self-referencing.

Common to the experiences of all of these entrepreneurs was that once early success seemed at hand, as their startups became viable businesses, their roles changed dramatically. They had to run companies, a different job from organizing a startup. Stebbins described the experience as "turning one path-breaking innovation into a company, then pivoting to managing a nonstop cycle of innovation to make the company grow." He smiled. "There had better be another innovation up ahead. The manager's job is to search for it."

Head learned this same lesson in a more difficult way, and much to his chagrin. When I asked why he had bought his way into Prince, he answered, "Selling Head Skis was a mistake." He had come to see himself as a good designer who hated the management side of building a company, but came to recognize that he still wanted in. Head told me, "If I had it to do over again, I would've stepped back from running Head and promoted myself to chief designer. I could've tried to learn tennis on the side. It would have been so much easier to have gotten to the big sweet spot in a new kind of racquet if I'd been inside my first company. There, my crazy ideas would've been seen in the context of the innovation culture that I'd built into the company."

Dyson has this figured out. He doesn't want the fun to end. From the outset, he saw his company's future as more than making vacuum cleaners. He wanted it to be a platform for innovation and, like many entrepreneurs, he continues to see his company as a work in progress. His latest startup is the Dyson Institute of Technology, an engineering university that opened its doors in 2017 on his company's large campus in Wiltshire, England. The twenty-five students in the inaugural class pay no tuition—they actually receive a salary—as they combine rigorous academic engineering studies with the opportunity to work with Dyson's engineers in England, Singapore, and Malaysia. Dyson is an indefatigable innovator-entrepreneur, always wanting to tackle and solve new problems.

This fluid reality may explain why it is that Dyson, Head, Kasbar, and Stebbins never started their endeavors with business plans. They weren't even sure that what they were toiling to achieve was a "company," they were just sure that they had really good ideas. Head disliked planning, perhaps because he found most management prescriptions "wrongheaded, because innovation and planning are not compatible." In one conversation in his study at home, surrounded by early versions of his skis, Head pointed to the first pair to have steel edges that bound the laminated layers together. After this model was introduced, Head learned that the edges made turning so much easier that skiers called them "cheaters." For Head, finding a property in his skis that he didn't envision and didn't design for, was pure magic. "Invention is a funny thing. While you're searching for something, you may stumble upon something else that proves vastly more important." He added, "Innovation is the gift that comes back to those who persevere. You can only improve your product when you have one."

# CHAPTER 6

# Big Companies Can Be Schools for Startups

At the dawn of the industrial revolution, sociologist Max Weber observed that, as companies grow and mature, they create internal rule-making bureaucracies that make innovation more and more difficult. Some established companies, however, are known to produce innovative products year after year. Among them are Amazon, Apple, BMW, GE, HP, IBM, Intel, Procter & Gamble, Medtronic, Nike, and Toyota. These companies also produce a constant stream of former employees who start companies; they are schools for entrepreneurs. Steve Wozniak so loved how much he was learning at Hewlett-Packard that Steve Jobs, who had worked for the game maker Atari, had to beg him to quit so that they could start Apple. Weber knew that what he called the "spirit of capitalism" created a counterforce to bureaucracy, one that causes big companies to spin out startups, some of which have proved to have more potential for success than their parents.[1]

The entrepreneurs you are about to meet launched their companies after careers in big companies. Their stories tell how much they learned about doing business that became essential when they unexpectedly found themselves starting companies. In each case, these entrepreneurs took away rich sets of lessons and experiences that proved crucial to their success.

Art Ciocca was inspecting grapes in a Napa Valley vineyard, 2,500 miles from his New York office, when he had an "E.T., phone home" moment. Ciocca was president of The Wine Group, a subsidiary of the Coca-Cola Bottling Company of New York. A friend had called saying that he'd heard that Coke was selling Art's business. Art couldn't believe it. He had just pulled off a three-year turnaround, receiving kudos and bonuses from Coke's board.

Coke's CEO confirmed the news, telling Ciocca that, the next day, the company's board would vote to sell The Wine Group. Besides feeling betrayed, he was devastated for another reason. "My team had worked so hard to get things turned around. Just as we were taking off, Coke decided to get rid of us. The great team I had built so carefully would never survive an acquisition by a big wine company."

Ciocca flew to New York that night. He argued to the board that the demand for wine would double every five years and that the soft-drink market, where Coke faced intense competition for its traditional products, didn't hold such promise. When one director said that Coke should never have gotten into wine in the first place, and that it had nothing to do with soft drinks, Ciocca surprised himself saying, "If you think so little of The Wine Group's future, then I'll buy it."

As soon as the meeting was over he flew back to San Francisco to talk with the only banker he knew. His banker told me that Ciocca's first question at breakfast the next morning was, "What's a leveraged buyout?" Ciocca learned that he would have to persuade investors to back him with enough money to meet Coke's best offer from another buyer, likely a giant beverage company with a strong balance sheet. For any one of them, buying Coke's wine business would be a routine acquisition.

Ciocca, however, had an advantage. He had remade The Wine Group and knew every aspect of its business. He had built a great team, established strong supply and distribution relationships, and overseen substantial growth. Ciocca announced that he would leave The Wine Group if it was sold to someone else. He got the support of lenders and bought the business.

## The Making of an Entrepreneur

Ciocca grew up in a close-knit Italian-American family in the Hudson Valley. As a teenager, his grandfather taught him how to tend grapes, and, in the fall, make the family's wine for the coming year. In college, he studied biology, thinking that he might follow in his father's footsteps as a doctor. After college, however, he was drafted and served three years in the military. As a Navy officer, Ciocca was stationed in Brooklyn and studied for his MBA at night.

His first job, with General Foods, took him to San Jose. Ciocca fell in love with California, especially its beautiful wine country. He quit when the company decided to move him to its New York headquarters, taking another job in San Francisco. Three years later, he went to work for Gallo Brothers, then a winery selling blended red wine in glass gallon jugs.

When Ciocca joined Gallo in the 1970s, enjoying wine with meals was not a common experience for Americans. Compared with today, California wine production was a cottage industry. Ciocca's job was to grow the market for Gallo, which meant understanding how to get more people to drink wine. He looks back on working closely with Ernest Gallo as a great piece of luck. "He was the best role model I could have had. Gallo was an extraordinary entrepreneur leading a small winery with a vision that, at the time, no one else in California saw. He worked day and night, making Gallo from a wine mostly consumed by Italian-Americans into a product that any American would want to drink."

Gallo was, however, a family business. Despite helping double its sales, Ciocca knew his career prospects were limited. His growing visibility in the wine industry resulted in his being recruited by Coke New York to head its fine beverage business, The Wine Group. "Coke's wine business was losing money. I knew it would be an overwhelming grind for three years, including commuting back and forth to California, but I was sure I could make The Wine Group profitable. If I pulled it off, I thought, someday I might run all of Coke."

It was just as The Wine Group turned profitable that Coke had second thoughts about running a business not directly related to what consultants call a company's "core competency." Coke was losing market to Pepsi. To efficiently compete, it would have to invest in new, more efficient plants and crank up its advertising. Suddenly, Coke's management saw its wine business as a distraction.

Ciocca knew that he was taking a big risk when he bought The Wine Group, but he did not fully know what that might include. Just as he completed his purchase, the economy crashed. Interest rates went to nearly nineteen percent. Ciocca, then in his midforties, owned a new company that had twenty-six times more debt than he had projected as first-year income. Worse, demand for wine was dropping as the economic downturn continued.

Within the year, however, Ciocca caught a lucky break. A bumper harvest resulted in much lower grape prices than he had forecast. The Wine Group had a chance to make money. But the company faced a different problem. Not looking forward to competition, several big wineries launched aggressive advertising campaigns aimed at taking market share from The Wine Group's products. His company, deep in debt, could not respond in kind.

Ciocca knew he couldn't survive by making better wines less expensively. He had to invent new products that would appeal to mass markets. With the team he had held together, Ciocca bet on an idea that changed everything. By mixing cheaper wines with fruit juice, The Wine Group became a big player in a craze now all but forgotten: wine coolers. In its second year, the company shipped one million cases. Sales doubled the next year. Ciocca used the profits to pay down debt, which allowed him to set the stage for more innovation.

Ciocca recalls that the key lesson was to keep innovating rather than doing more marketing. "Innovation was the critical component of The Wine Group's success. Every year, thirty-five percent of our profit comes from products that didn't exist three years before." Since he purchased and restarted The Wine Group thirty years ago, it has grown to twenty-five times its original size. Its brands include Franzia, Concannon, Almaden, Corbett Canyon, Inglenook, Foghorn, and many others. Today, Ciocca's company is the world's third-largest producer. In 2013, its Cupcake label, developed with young professional women in mind, became America's best selling premium wine.

## Spin-Out Entrepreneurs

Ciocca never saw himself becoming an entrepreneur. He was climbing the corporate ladder, hoping to run a big company, when an unexpected situation changed everything. His experience, however, is more common than you might think. Research has now shown us that mature large companies cradle thousands of spin-out businesses.

Taken together, big companies produce more innovation than

they can ever absorb. Existing companies, not entrepreneurial startups nor universities, are the single largest source of innovation in our economy. Ninety percent of all patents issued every year go to established companies. IBM, for example, received more than seven thousand patents in 2015, two percent of all those awarded. As large companies continually adjust strategic direction in response to emerging innovations, one result is an ongoing outflow of operating units and the jettisoning of potential creative initiatives that no longer are seen as key to a company's future. Coke New York once saw wine making as a way to diversify and grow. But, faced with mounting pressures on its core business, it retreated to accepted managerial wisdom, "Do more of what you're good at."

About ten percent of all new ventures result from their founder's experience with their last employer. In this chapter, we will meet other entrepreneurs, none of whom expected to leave their employers, and certainly not to own startups. Like Ciocca, some became entrepreneurs by owning businesses their employers had decided were no longer important to the parent's future. Others, frustrated that their employer refused to develop an idea that they were sure held great promise, quit to build companies on those ideas. Both are called "spinout" entrepreneurs.

## Blowing the Future

At fifty-four, Fred Valerino became a first-time entrepreneur. Much like Ciocca, the circumstances came as a complete surprise. Valerino had worked for Lamson Manufacturing since college. The company had invented pneumatic tubes in the late nineteenth century as the state-of-the-art means of moving sales slips and cash around department stores. Most big stores had Lamson systems; at the beginning of the twentieth century the company had installed thirty-nine miles of tubing at Harrods in London. Today, the same technology can be seen in every Home Depot. Cash is sent to and from the manager's office in cylindrical carriers, pushed along in metal tubes by compressed air.

As Valerino celebrated his twenty-fifth year of employment, the nation's biggest maker of bank vaults bought Lamson. Diebold had supplied safes and more modern technology to the banking industry since eight hundred of its vaults survived the great Chicago fire of 1871, and it decided that it needed Lamson's pneumatic tube systems for drive-through banking, a service innovation that had come with suburbanization.

Diebold, by acquiring Lamson, found itself the largest supplier of pneumatic tubes to hospitals. Since 1904, when Lamson installed its first system at the Mayo Clinic, connecting operating rooms to labs so that specimens could be analyzed in the middle of surgeries, hundreds of hospitals also had installed pneumatic systems to move drugs, patient records, and billing information. After the merger, Valerino was put in charge of Diebold's hospital customers.

Diebold, however, was never comfortable serving hospitals; its DNA was banking. When Diebold decided to become the dominant maker of automatic-teller machines, and to manage the 24/7 communications between ATMs and banks, it decided that pneumatic systems in hospitals were no longer among its core competencies. In fact, many hospitals were abandoning their antiquated tube systems.

As Ciocca had done with Coke, Valerino pleaded with Diebold to see healthcare as a way to transition the company to a bigger market in the future. He argued that the demand for healthcare would grow as the population aged and healthcare coverage expanded. Pneumatic tubes would be needed to move more lab tests and drugs in hospitals, nursing homes, and newly forming surgery centers. Valerino also was sure that the demand for Diebold's banking technology would slow as the cashless economy continued to evolve.

Despite his advocacy, Diebold was so eager to end its healthcare business that it proposed that Valerino take the business in exchange for maintaining existing customer-service contracts until they expired. He was offered an operating business and a little income.

But Valerino's "free" startup came with a daunting price. While he had no debt, he didn't have a competitive product. Before sending an item in a tube, users still had to adjust numbered brass rings on each carrier to steer it to the intended destination. This was the same mechanical method that had been used for a century, and it was far from perfect. A carrier containing a blood sample, drugs, or paperwork had only an eighty percent chance of getting to the right place on the first try. While hospitals were using computers for transmitting lab results back to caregivers, specimens still had to get to the lab. Some hospitals had reverted to using human couriers.

Fortunately, Valerino also got lucky within a year of starting Pevco, his new company. Hospitals came under fire for mistakes that were killing patients. One sensational study linked four hundred inpatient deaths a day to mistakes, including mixed-up lab samples and drugs administered to the wrong patients. Newspapers compared the problem to the equivalent of three 747s crashing every two days.[2] Valerino knew that if he could build a zero-defects tube system that never mixed up lab samples or sent nurses the wrong drugs, his new company just might survive.

He approached a hospital in rural Maryland with a make-or-break proposition. The hospital agreed to buy a new system if Pevco could provide ninety-eight percent destination accuracy. If not, the new system would be free. Valerino designed a new guidance system using computers and bar codes for every carrier, continuously tracking the containers as they traveled from place to place. His first installation, his bet-the-ranch deal, delivered one hundred percent destination accuracy the minute the system went live. He had a happy customer who then served as a reference to other hospitals. Valerino had invented a new life for pneumatic communication in healthcare.

He had bet on innovation to revive a century-old product. Today, Pevco holds nearly one hundred patents and has built two factories, one in Baltimore, the other in Houston. A quarter of America's 3,200 hospitals have installed Pevco systems to save labor and reduce potential liability related to mixing up specimens and drugs. In 2015, Valerino's company installed the biggest system in the world, connecting six hospitals in Houston.

## From Outer Space to Shelves at GNC

David Kyle worked in an industrial research laboratory at the aerospace giant Martin Marietta. A Ph.D. in biochemistry, like the scientists he worked with, he had turned down a professorship to work on cutting-edge science. His lab's mission was to develop algae as a waste-disposal catalyst, a food supply, and a source of oxygen to sustain life on a space station.

Two years into this research, Martin Marietta decided to return to its historic competency—building military aircraft. Its space lab was no longer to be part of the company's future. Fearing that he would be out of a job, Kyle agreed to return to Cornell as a professor. Martin Marietta, however, had a different idea, one that changed his life. The company proposed that he and two colleagues transition their lab to a free-standing company. As Kyle remembers it, "Martin Marietta was giving us the nicest good-bye possible."

The arrangement included giving the trio all their lab's equipment, and money to pay their salaries for a year.

The hitch was that they would be starting a research laboratory with no customers and nothing to sell. Kyle and his partners would have to redirect their research to find an earthly use for algae, one that could make money. Each believed commercial products were possible but knew that their task, which would involve experimenting with thousands of strains of algae, would be enormous. Their entrepreneurial moment was at hand. The three pooled $25,000 from savings and incorporated Martek.

Immediately, they focused on fifty algae strains that they suspected might have commercial uses. Their first research contract involved finding a way to convert fat molecules in chicken feed to produce low-cholesterol eggs. As a byproduct of their work on chickens, Martek came up with its first product, a vegetable oil many times more stable than the oil derived from petroleum. Selling for a few thousand dollars an ounce, it was used, among other things, for lubricating bearings on precision instruments like gyroscopes. Experimenting with fermenting one strain of algae after another with various mixtures of nitrates, phosphates, and carbon dioxide, they were soon making food colorings and fluorescing agents used in diagnostics.

Initially, Martek scraped by making such specialty products and on research grants from the federal government. Using Small Business Innovation Research (SBIR) Awards, which are grants to help high-tech startups develop viable commercial products, Kyle's team discovered how to generate docosahexaenoic acid (DHA), from algae. DHA, discovered in the 1920s, was the first of the "good" fats, necessary for heart health. Prior to discovering how to make DHA from algae, it was extracted from animal and fish sources, and invariably contaminated, so DHA's benefits were compromised. The growing community of consumers wanting organic products opened a market for Martek.

In order to produce DHA and other algae-based supplements at scale, the company needed large facilities to continuously ferment its products. Several venture funds provided capital, allowing the company to buy two abandoned breweries. In 1993, eight years after it was started, the company sold shares to the public. Martek became the world's principal manufacturer of algae-based food supplements, supplying thousands of companies around the world. The company also developed its own supplement brands in conjunction with General Nutrition Centers (GNC) stores, and developed private label brands for other outlets, including Walmart.

In 2010, twenty-five years after its three partners had put up $25,000, they sold Martek to an international ingredient company for $1.1 billion.

## Frustrated Corporate Innovators

Ciocca, Valerino, and Kyle might not fit the popular image of entrepreneurs. To some they look like executives who, because of a shift in an employer's strategy, had a chance to own a business that they already were running. Each could have ignored the opportunity, moved to another company, or, with a Ph.D., like Kyle, gone back to teaching. Instead, they all took up the entrepreneur's challenge—developing a vision, creating an innovation, assuming enormous risk, and persevering to achieve scale. Starting small or lean was not in the cards for them. Ciocca was like David compared to the Goliaths of the wine industry; Valerino took over a business with a broken technology; and Kyle knew that the lab he had been given could never make money with the space station as its only customer.

Ciocca told me, "I never thought of myself as an entrepreneur. When I started in business, the word just wasn't used. I knew, though, that the people who made a difference—a lesson I learned from Ernest Gallo—were those who saw that risk-taking was necessary to success. It's the hallmark of what entrepreneurs do. But, I think it takes a blend of knowing what the boundaries of your risk are and then trusting that your vision can make your business grow. To do that you have to keep pushing into the unknown, which means constantly inventing products that will define your company. So, like every successful entrepreneur, I managed risk by focusing on innovation."

Valerino's recollection of his early days at Pevco parallel those of iconic entrepreneurs. He didn't take a salary for three years. He burned up all his savings paying suppliers. He inherited a unionized workforce. "I had to pay the union dues on time, or else I got a visit." He rented a tiny house as his office. Looking back, he laughs that his competitors showed pictures of his headquarters to dissuade potential customers. "If I wasn't living the life of an entrepreneur, I don't know who was. I bet the whole company on a dare that I could build a perfect system."

Kyle saw Martek's challenge as making a commercial product by using his team's incomplete but cutting edge knowledge about culturing algae. There were enormous manufacturing risks involved in buying old breweries to ferment at scale. Martek took twelve years to become profitable. "Many nights, falling to sleep, I thought about how simple and secure my life would have been if I'd gone back to teaching."

For Ciocca, Valerino, and Kyle, their entrepreneurial opportunity was not of their own making. Like all companies, Coke, Diebold, and Martin Marietta constantly weigh the strategic importance of various parts of their business relative to changing circumstances.

Whether right or wrong, they dispose of business units they believe are peripheral to their futures. Every year, large companies sell thousands of operating units, many times to employees.

The same large companies produce even more of another type of spinout entrepreneur: employees who leave to immediately begin work on an innovative idea that they had while working at the company, but in which they couldn't provoke any interest, or sometimes even elicit any response, from management. Entrepreneurs who resign their positions to start new companies often are frustrated that their employers could not appreciate the growth potential of their insights and innovative ideas for their employer's future.

## Innovation Must Find a Home

Two of the best-known frustrated innovators, who valiantly tried to persuade two employers to leverage a discovery into explosive growth, were Robert Noyce and Gordon Moore. Both began their careers at Bell Labs, perhaps the best known industrial-research facility in history. There, they worked for William Shockley, the Nobel Prize physicist who invented the transistor. Overnight, the vacuum tube, which had made radio, television, radar, and computers possible, was obsolete. Noyce and Moore left Bell with Shockley, joining his startup and believing that he was committed to advancing and manufacturing semiconductors. After two years, it became apparent to them that Shockley was more interested in further research than in grabbing what Noyce and Moore saw as the golden ring in semiconductors.

The pair turned to Fairchild Camera Corporation to bankroll a new company, Fairchild Semiconductor, that would make transistors and assemble them into microchips. Located in Mountain

View, California, they were surrounded by other startups working on applications of microchips to all kinds of new devices, including computers. Noyce and Moore came to see that the demand was much bigger than even they had imagined; they forecasted that it would double every two years. As they saw it, their company could produce huge profits for Fairchild Camera if it would build a big enough factory. Fairchild Camera, however, wasn't interested; it refused to take the risk involved. Noyce and Moore quit once again, this time to create Intel, which became the world's largest manufacturer of microchips—the "inside" of many of the world's personal computers. Intel is now seventy-five times bigger than Fairchild.

Another ubiquitous technology that is part of all of our lives evolved in much the same way. Gary Burrell, the head designer at the King Radio Company in Kansas City, hired Min Kao, a newly minted Ph.D. in electrical engineering. Using semiconductors, together they were designing new communication and navigation systems for small airplanes made by King's customers, Cessna, Piper, and Beechcraft. When AlliedSignal (now Honeywell) acquired King, the pair was tasked with continued development of top-secret guidance systems for missiles carrying nuclear warheads. These systems were being redesigned to use newly available satellite signals to pinpoint the locations of potential targets that might be anywhere on earth.

Burrell and Kao came to understand that the global positioning system (GPS) used to guide missiles could be used to improve navigation for airplanes and ships. Try as they might to explain the market potential of GPS signals in such commercial applications, AlliedSignal believed its future success was tied to building weapons systems for the Defense Department. In 1989, when the government permitted civilian use of satellite-positioning signals, Burrell and Kao left to start a new company.

Garmin, a combination of their first names, introduced its first product a year later, at the 1990 Marine Technology Exposition in Chicago. The GPS 100, a navigation aid for ships, was an instant success. They left the convention with five thousand orders and a conviction that their next product should be geared to a mass consumer market. Burrell and Kao set to work on a hand-held GPS device, the Garmin eTrex H, introduced in 1991. Garmin grabbed headlines, and a huge market, when news spread that U.S. servicemen were using their personal "Garmins" in combat during the Gulf War. Today, all of us have Garmin technology in our lives, supporting the mapping applications on our mobile devices, telling us that our missing luggage is in Brazil when it should be in Tulsa, and showing how many feet above sea level we are on the mountain we're climbing.

## Before Starting Your Own, Work for Another Company

Nearly ninety percent of all entrepreneurs have worked for other employers before starting their companies. Embryonic entrepreneurs cannot help but absorb lessons working for established companies that can prove useful as they start their own. If you are an aspiring entrepreneur, what should you do to get the most from such an experience?

### Work for an Innovative Company

Ewing Kauffman delighted in knowing that many new companies, at least fifteen, were created by former employees of Marion Labs. He viewed his company as a nursery for other entrepreneurs. He also believed that, as long as people were leaving with great ideas for new companies, provided they didn't compete with Marion, his company was fostering the entrepreneurial spirit that he tried to preserve even as his company grew.

---

### Learn the Innovation Process

But being in an innovative environment is not enough. An aspiring entrepreneur needs to pay close attention to the process by which companies develop new products. How does the company's research shape new products? How does market feedback from the company's sales force inform evolving product design? How does the company decide to spend capital on new machines or plants?

Also, you should study the pace at which growth is happening among various products within the company. As innovation accelerates in one product line, those products or divisions with slower growth or higher risk often are sold off. Ciocca and Valerino found themselves in just such situations. If they look, employees in big companies get to see the tug and pull of how companies decide to advance one product at the expense of others. Spinout entrepreneurs often can seize opportunities arising when companies shift their production mix.

### Appreciate Scale

Many entrepreneurs without the experience of working in big companies unconsciously limit their ambitions regarding how big their startup might become. One reason is that many have never even seen a big factory or the inside of a huge warehouse, venues that serve as reference points for scale.

As a young Wall Street banker, Jeff Bezos, founder of Amazon, which now owns giant warehouses in nearly every state, had visited companies, toured factories, and seen complex and large-scale logistics at work. Bezos had analyzed financial reports that described the scope and scale of really large companies. This experience allowed Bezos to imagine Amazon becoming a giant company even while it was a startup.

## Acquire Industry Knowledge

Very few spinout entrepreneurs start companies outside of the industries in which they work. The obvious reason is that they have acquired specific industrial knowledge. After ten years of experience working for Gallo and running Coke's wine business, Ciocca knew every detail of growing grapes, making wine, running a bottle factory, and distributing and selling. When the opportunity appeared, he had the necessary experience to buy and run The Wine Group as a startup.

Industries are defined by products, the technologies related to making them, and the customers who buy them. Competitors use the same raw materials, processes, and, mostly, the same sales channels. People who have worked in one company for a long time learn not just the ways of that company but the rules of the industry. Executives within an industry often move from one company to another. They are not hired because they bring a competitor's secrets, but because they know the common culture of the industry. Someone working at Macy's may be valuable to Target because he knows the general operating rules for retailing; he doesn't have to learn the business.

This is the same reason that entrepreneurs starting companies hire people with industry experience. If you start a candy-bar company, someone who has worked at Mars comes knowing how to source cocoa, make candy at scale, the idiosyncrasies of candy wholesaling, and how effective marketing can bring customers to your product.

## Develop Industry Networks

Working in a big company inevitably produces a wide set of contacts and friends in the company and industry. These networks are valuable to spinout entrepreneurs in many ways. Ciocca knew people everywhere in the wine industry when he started The Wine Group, from grape farmers to liquor store owners. When he left Coke with his new company he could draw on the goodwill he had amassed. Ciocca told me, "Without industry connections I wouldn't have had much of a chance of even buying grapes."

Valerino fondly remembers the suppliers that he had used at Diebold extending Pevco credit when he couldn't pay for parts. Burrell and Kao, because of their connections in the defense industry, had presumed credibility when they approached shipping companies who, seeing the advantages of using geopositioning technology, were ready to buy their new navigation products.

## Business Planning and Spinout Entrepreneurs

Every big company has teams of MBAs working on strategy. Coke, Diebold, Martin Marietta, Fairchild, and Allied Signal had up-to-date written business plans. Each contemplated leveraging the company's past successes, its core competencies, into future growth. None, however, anticipated the events that led Ciocca, Valerino, Kyle, Burrell, and Kao to break away, several becoming bigger than their parents. AlliedSignal, for example, could not see the potential of what Burrell and Kao described—it was outside their strategy of weapons research and production.

The president of a publicly traded company once told me, "Of course, we have a business plan. If an acquirer shows up, I'm ready. But, I keep it locked in my desk. If I circulated it inside the company, people would work toward its goals at the expense of seeing all the opportunities our customers keep presenting to us. And, I never want someone here to think that they would have to start their own company because we wouldn't treat their idea as a potentially transformative innovation."

## What Employers Can Learn from Spinout Entrepreneurs

Most spinout entrepreneurs never intended to start companies. Most were loyal employees. Their arguments on behalf of expanding their product lines or developing a particular innovation genuinely were motivated by wanting to see their employer become more successful and profitable.

Economist Albert Hirschman, in an attempt to understand why some firms don't grow as fast as others, studied the behavior of employees who saw the future of their firms differently from their bosses. In his book *Exit, Voice, and Loyalty*, Hirschman argued that many people who left companies were frustrated that their former employer couldn't see how bright its future would be if it embraced the vision or innovation that they had proposed.[3] Hirschman saw them as disappointed that their work could not contribute to their employer's future success.

Valerino's loyalty to Diebold continues all these years later. He still recalls how reluctant he was to leave. "Diebold was a great company. I should have made all this money for them." He continued, "All it took was faith that pneumatic tubes had a big future in hospitals." Ciocca recalls with a tinge of regret, "Coke just couldn't see wine as its future. It could have been the biggest wine company in the world." In retrospect, Ciocca, Valerino, Kyle, Noyce, Moore, and Burrell and Kao, all were innovation scouts, trying to find the path for their former companies. In reality, they each were becoming entrepreneurs in the process.

# CHAPTER 7

# Copycat Entrepreneurs

Scott Norton and Mark Ramadan, seniors in the class of 2008 at Brown, were studying international relations and economics. Neither had taken a course in entrepreneurship, so they weren't under the gun to come up with a great business plan. Somehow, one night, their casual talk turned to starting a new company.

The unexpected prompt was a four-year-old story in *The New Yorker*, in which Malcolm Gladwell posed what they saw as a challenge. Gladwell had done an extensive story on the nature of taste, reporting that some products, including Coke, Pepsi, and Sara Lee Pound Cake, had "amplitude," a rare quality reflecting a special combination of flavors. Such products resonate with consumer tastes so uniquely that they occupy categories all by themselves. Hellmann's, for example, is, for most Americans, synonymous with mayonnaise.

Gladwell cited another example, Heinz ketchup. He told the story of how it had been conceived by Henry J. Heinz in his kitchen in Pittsburgh. Prior to Heinz, ketchup was made at home. Housewives cooked scrap tomatoes, making sauce to flavor soup, fish, and meat. Heinz introduced the first commercial ketchup in 1906.

He used perfect tomatoes because they made a better-tasting product with a longer shelf life. The taste of his product was an instant hit; both sweet and tangy, Heinz's recipe was a thick sauce compared to watery homemade ketchup. Together, its taste and consistency achieved the illusive property of a category-defining product. After a while, homemade ketchup no longer tasted right. Gladwell wrote that, because of the magic of amplitude, the flavor of Heinz ketchup was impossible to beat. Despite other food companies having tried for decades, no one could dethrone Heinz from its dominant market position.

Gladwell's story also recounted how Grey Poupon had been managed into a major brand in the 1970s. A French-style Dijon mustard, made in Connecticut since 1946, Grey Poupon had never enjoyed anything but a tiny share of the gourmet market. Mustard in America was a choice between two colors, bright yellow (French's) or yellow-brown (Gulden's). As Julia Child spread the gospel of French cooking with her PBS television show in the 1960s, marketing professionals saw an opportunity. They reinvented Grey Poupon. The makeover involved using a large-mouthed glass jar, stenciled with the French flag. It was to appeal to higher-income consumers and its television campaign, one of the most famous ever, featured English aristocrats passing a jar of Grey Poupon from one Rolls Royce to another. The advertising experts were in pursuit of "snob appeal." Within a decade, Grey Poupon was the most powerful mustard brand in the country, selling at more than twice the price of its competitors.

After reading the piece, Norton and Ramadan mused about inventing a new ketchup and trying their own variation of the Grey Poupon marketing strategy. Maybe they could upend Heinz's hold on the American ketchup market. After graduation they went their separate ways, taking entry-level positions in a bank and a brokerage firm. But they continued to muse about a new ketchup company. Two years later, both quit their jobs and went to work formulating a recipe that was even thicker than Heinz's.

Having created a distinctive product, they set out to devise an innovative branding strategy. Their objective was to build a customer community, people who related to their brand as loyalists, the way drivers become loyal to cars made by certain manufacturers. They invented a fictional globe-trotting Englishman to give his name to their product and company. A graduate of Oxford, who had been stationed throughout the British Empire, Sir Kensington was famous for collecting exotic recipes. Once, so the story was told, he whipped up the precursor of modern-day ketchup while entertaining Catherine the Great. Norton and Ramadan were lucky enough to discover the "long lost" recipe in, of all places, the Brown University library.

The image of Sir Kensington, a mustachioed insouciant gentleman wearing an Edwardian collar, top hat, and monocle, appears on every jar, above the company's motto "A Divine Alternative." The company's product is packed in distinctive glass jars; they can't be squirted, only spooned. Its website presents Sir Kensington's history, prompting customers to retell the product's clever backstory.

Norton and Ramadan debuted Sir Kensington's at the New York Fancy Foods show in 2010. Williams-Sonoma and Dean & DeLuca ordered on the spot. Within a month, Dean & DeLuca was back for more. Whole Foods, where shelf space is a new food company's dream, wanted to carry the brand. Norton and Ramadan also sold directly to upscale New York restaurants and hotels, including the Ritz-Carlton, as a way of introducing their brand to affluent travelers who then would ask for it back home. In their first year of operations, Sir Kensington's sold ten thousand jars of ketchup.

Seven years later, Sir Kensington's is in grocery stores all over the country. The company has developed three other products: mayonnaise, mustard, and a vegan mayonnaise-like spread, Fabanaise, which is made with water used to process chickpeas. With sales growing by over one hundred percent annually, the company was purchased in 2017 by Unilever.

Sir Kensington's success is related to copying two ideas. Norton and Ramadan did not invent ketchup; they created a new recipe for a staple of the American diet. Likewise, they devised a marketing strategy that was presaged by Grey Poupon some forty years earlier. This chapter examines how copying existing ideas serves as an alternative to starting a company with a unique innovation.

## Copied Ideas

In fact, like Norton and Ramadan, most entrepreneurs are "replicative," that is, they take an existing product or idea and make it better. This is what Howard Head and James Dyson did. This process of incremental or iterative improvement is the basis of almost all innovation. Innovation proceeds in phases; inventors take what exists and create accretive combinations. Often an innovation comes down to having brought existing things together in a way never before seen. Dozens of search-engine startups existed before Google. The company copied others, becoming successful by analyzing individual searches for patterns that could be sold to advertisers.

The notion of emulating others' ideas seems foreign to many people when they think about entrepreneurs and startups. This reaction is heavily influenced by the mythology of Silicon Valley— that every entrepreneur must invent a distinct, totally original, technology.

No invention, however, stands apart from history. This reality is nowhere more clearly demonstrated than by examining patents issued by the federal government for new products. As a condition of government recognizing an idea as intellectual property, thus granting the patent holder the exclusive right to commercially develop the idea for twenty years, it must be made public.

Today all the records of the Patent Office are online. These records serve as the best history of how technology develops; right there in front of you is the record of the evolving state of the art. Most of the time spent in securing a patent involves differentiating the applicant's idea from previously protected ideas. Every applicant must refer to existing patents to demonstrate that his idea is really new. Thousands of employees of global companies read patent applications professionally, trying to discern the trajectory of new technological developments. Their employers hire them because they know that their findings can prompt novel combinations of new discoveries with existing technologies, leading to successive innovations.

In this regard, patents serve a larger societal purpose. Although originally conceived as a means to protect the property rights of inventors to their ideas and products, the patent process actually stimulates the process of innovation itself. This effect was easier to visualize in the past. Prior to the 1920s, every patent application had to be accompanied by a physical model of the invention. These models were exquisitely rendered miniatures, so detailed that surviving ones are regarded as works of art. Limited to twelve by eight inches, some have tiny cast-iron frames, often holding smaller gears made of steel and brass. Others have very small steam valves that actually open and close.

Once a patent was granted, its model was displayed at the Patent Office in Washington. For decades, this collection was the most visited place in the capital. Would-be inventors from around the nation came to study the hand-crafted miniatures of Samuel Morse's telegraph key, John Deere's steel plow, and Edison's phonograph. George Westinghouse's air brake, descendants of which continue to stop every train in the world, could be studied as well as his earlier patents for seed drills that automated corn planting. Visitors could see Eliphalet Remington's model for an improved shotgun, which became every hunter and frontiersman's weapon of choice, and, separated by two decades, the model for the Remington type-writer that revolutionized business correspondence.

The Patent Museum served as a school for inventors. Visitors came from all over the country, intent on creating a new product. If they looked carefully, they took away with them the lesson that most inventions are incremental improvements to what already had been invented.

## Business Model Innovation

Today, one can see only a small collection of patent models in the Smithsonian. Two are preserved because of their extraordinary importance: Cyrus McCormick's reaper and Isaac Singer's sewing machine. Each machine was, in fact, a remarkable combination of previously patented ideas, all part of an irrepressible drive to mechanize harvesting and sewing for more efficient food and garment production. The reason that we see each as emblems of such technical importance has as much to do with the business models that McCormick and Singer developed, which made their respective companies so historically notable.

McCormick's reaper permitted farmers to harvest with many fewer hands, increasing their productivity many times over. As a result, farmers could own bigger farms and enjoy economies of scale. Of equal importance, harvesting became much faster, greatly reducing the risk of losing matured crops to incoming bad weather. Reapers were so expensive, however, that most farmers could not afford them.

To get his machine into the hands of customers, McCormick hit upon the idea of installment purchasing. McCormick's idea wasn't new; farmers had long used mortgages to pay for their land and houses. McCormick's company, International Harvester, operated much like a bank for the farmer's machinery. The underlying relationship of trust paid dividends for decades. Many farmers are still International Harvester loyalists for reasons reaching back to the company's help to their great-grandfathers.

Singer, by inventing the modern sewing machine, revolutionized an industry. But model evidence shows how close others had come to his design; his breakthrough actually is rather a minor improvement on several previous patents. Singer's machine, like McCormick's, was so expensive that few could afford to buy it. When sewing machines first appeared in the 1850s, each cost more than a seamstress' average annual wage. Singer borrowed McCormick's idea of installment buying, which greatly increased his sales. With growing demand, Singer continuously devised production efficiencies that caused the price of a machine to fall so quickly that, within just a few years, it was the equivalent of a month's wages.

## Inventing Entrepreneurial Partners

To reach a mass market, however, Singer faced a problem even more formidable than price. Customers had to be converted to the idea of machine sewing. Through all of history, clothes had been made at home and by hand, and for the wealthy, by skilled servants. Outside of the rarified privileged class, the skilled handiwork of sewing was a fundamental skill of a good housekeeper, and a competence that contributed to a woman's marital eligibility. The sewing machine, as a household appliance, had no predecessor. The idea of machines as labor-saving devices outside of factories was unknown. Singer's machine predated mass-produced vacuum cleaners and washing machines by nearly six decades. To most women, sewing other than by hand was unimaginable.

To expand his market, Singer had to invent a new business model, one that solved two problems never before encountered. First, he had to demonstrate to housewives the benefits of sewing by machine. To do this, he needed a national network of sewing schools. And, if his relatively complex machines were to be adopted, he had to ensure quick repairs were available. Singer's foot-pedal powered sewing machine was the first mass-marketed technology that required technical support.

Not able to finance the cost of building a national network of sewing schools and service centers, Singer created a profoundly important innovation. He would leverage the entrepreneurial ambitions of others to be his partners, to start businesses that were mutually supportive. Singer recruited entrepreneurs to run sewing schools, sell his machines, and provide repair service for their customers.

Singer gave the customer relationship to his partners, allowing him to concentrate on manufacturing. Aspiring entrepreneurs paid Singer a licensing fee to sell his machines and, in return, he provided them with exclusive sales territories and promoted the Singer brand with print advertising in national women's magazines.

Singer had invented the modern franchise. He accelerated his entrepreneurial ambitions by recruiting and training entrepreneurs who built businesses around his revolutionary product. Five decades later, Henry Ford copied Singer's distribution model, selling exclusive territory licenses to build a dealer network responsible for selling and servicing his cars.

This long history of symbiosis between innovator–entrepreneurs like Singer and Ford, and the entrepreneurs who owned nodes on their sales networks, is obscured by the modern king of franchising, Ray Kroc. Kroc worked for a small Illinois company where he sold machines capable of making five milkshakes at once. While most customers bought one machine at a time, a restaurant in San Bernardino, operated by Dick and Mac McDonald, bought eight. Curious, Kroc found his way to San Bernardino, California, to see who was making so many milkshakes. Arriving at McDonald's, Kroc knew he was seeing something different. The McDonald brothers had industrialized the production of hamburgers, fries, and milkshakes. They could produce an affordable, delicious meal in a matter of minutes, what we now know as fast food.

Around Southern California, McDonald's was already something of a legend. Before Kroc's visit, Keith J. Kramer and Matthew Burns had come to California to study the McDonald's system. Upon returning to Jacksonville, Florida, they started Insta-Burger, a chain that later was renamed Burger King. Glen Bell, a World War II veteran living in California, opened a stand selling hot dogs and hamburgers just down the street from the McDonalds' location. After watching the McDonald brothers' business grow, he decided to apply their system to what had become a local food craze. He opened his first Taco Bell in 1962. Unlike the hamburgers that McDonald's made, Bell had to introduce large parts of America to what, he joked, many people called "Tay-kohs." But, as his sixth year closed, there were 325 Taco Bells across the western states.

It was Kroc, however, who in 1955 talked the McDonalds into a national franchise license. Within seven years, Kroc had bought out the brothers and had built a franchise network of 230 stores. Kroc recruited first-time entrepreneurs, independent owner–operators, to become his partners. He recognized McDonald's as an innovation that could be copied all over the country. He recruited franchisees as partners to whom he sold localized rights to his great idea, and worked hard to see that they would prosper with him.

## Co-entrepreneurship

Like practically every fast-food franchisee, Bob Carlucci became an entrepreneur using someone else's idea. Growing up in Boston, he wanted nothing more than to be a musician. After high school he enrolled in the New England Conservatory of Music. When his father died unexpectedly, Carlucci dropped out to help his mother, who worked as a seamstress, support his three younger brothers. He got a night job at a General Electric factory. Along the way he bought two candy vending machines and installed them in the pool hall he managed on the side.

Having concluded that a classical music career was out, and hating his work at GE, Carlucci decided that starting a business was his best path forward. He built his first company on the only experience he had: vending. Reading the *Boston Globe* one morning, he discovered that Lechmere, a local department store, was planning to open fifteen auto-service centers. On an impulse, Carlucci wrote to the company, proposing that he provide vending to each of its new stores. Miraculously, the store's purchasing manager asked for a meeting. Carlucci had cards printed indicating that he was the sales manager for R&R vending. The interview ended with Lechmere asking him to bid. He responded with a few paragraphs, describing a company that didn't exist.

In a meeting a few weeks later, Carlucci was asked to install soft-drink and coffee machines in the company's new auto centers and also its warehouse and employee cafeteria. Driving home in a cold sweat, he remembers saying to himself, "I am a fraud." He was only twenty-three; his corporate assets consisted of two vending machines and what his mother would call "a lot of nerve."

When Carlucci explained his situation to his uncle, an accountant, and the only family member who knew anything about business, he got a crash course in how to build a spreadsheet projecting sales and costs. Next, Carlucci's uncle took him to meet the president of the local bank. After hearing about Carlucci's opportunity, the bank's president agreed to lend him money to get started. More important, he said, "We will meet once a week and I will teach you how to do business."

Within a decade, Carlucci was providing corporate vending as far away as Washington, D.C. As he looked into the future, however, he saw an industry heading for trouble. He knew that selling cigarettes from vending machines, the industry's most profitable item, was soon to be outlawed by government. Carlucci wanted out of the vending business, so he began to explore franchises. "I knew I had gotten pretty good at running a business, but I didn't have any particularly great new ideas. Inventing a new product and building a business around it involved more risk than I wanted to take."

At the time, Taco Bell was developing a national market. Carlucci told me, "Growing up in Boston, I never ate a taco; I don't think I had ever seen one before." He approached Taco Bell proposing a statewide territory license for Maryland. Instead, Taco Bell offered him one location close to Annapolis. After building and running it successfully, he got the chance to own several more. Carlucci remembers being turned down by one banker who said, "I think this franchise won't survive; tacos give me gas."

Today, Carlucci owns seventy restaurants in seven states and the District of Columbia. He employs 1,400 people. When I asked Carlucci about his secret to success, he responded instantly, "I used the idea that Taco Bell had invented." He went on, "I could see the idea worked. I became an entrepreneur because Glen Bell had a great idea. He invented the idea of Taco Bell, I was one of hundreds he invited to follow him."

The story of Carlucci is not unique. Many entrepreneurs build scale businesses by owning many franchises. In fact, the majority of McDonald's owners operate more than one franchise. C. Howard Wilkins Jr. provides another example. Six years after graduating from Yale, he bought a Pizza Hut franchise, a concept recently invented by two students at Wichita State University in his hometown in Kansas. Within two years, he had acquired sixteen stores in Kentucky. A few years later, he sold his stores to the franchisor, becoming Pizza Hut's Vice President for International Operations. In 1970, he started Pizza Corporation of America, operating 270 Pizza Huts as well as other franchises in the U.S. and around the world, and a property development corporation to support his expansion. Later in his career, he served as America's ambassador to the Netherlands, where he was famed for spreading the story of how important entrepreneurs are to America's economy.

## Entrepreneurial Synergy

New franchises account for nearly forty percent of all new business started each year. Success among strong franchises such as Jimmy John's sandwiches, Sport Clips Haircuts, and Auntie Anne's pretzels is very high. Nearly everyone who owns one of the two hundred strongest franchised brands succeeds: Five-year survival rates are over ninety-five percent.

Curiously, very few university business schools teach even one course about franchising. College students can major in entrepreneurship without ever considering a franchise. This situation reflects the view of most business professors, who do not think of franchisees as real entrepreneurs. As we have seen, their definition, heavily influenced by venture investors, focuses principally on innovator–entrepreneurs, originators of the idea for their own startups. To many professors, it seems building a business with someone else's concept disqualifies franchisees as real entrepreneurs.

When I asked Carlucci about this he told me that every franchise owner sees himself as an entrepreneur. "We all start businesses. The only difference is we become part of building out someone else's idea. I've had to make every one of my businesses successful. Like many entrepreneurs, I had someone else's money at stake. I call that taking risk. While my venture capital came from banks, I was playing with someone else's money. I was up to my eyelids in debt. If I didn't make my first Taco Bell work, I would have been bankrupt. I had to solve all the unexpected problems every entrepreneur faces. In my case, I had to learn about cooking, construction, become an expert on wastewater management in parking lots, and the complexities of keeping a semiskilled, minimum-wage workforce motivated. I solved bigger problems, too. I diversified my franchise base, operating hotels, and other restaurant brands. Eventually, I bought a bank to make expansion easier."

Successful franchisors, the originators of the idea around which the franchise is built, understand that they must create entrepreneurs like themselves if they are to be successful. They knit together networks of entrepreneurs to reach scale. Without recruiting local entrepreneurs who own their outlets and operate as independent businesses, household brands such as Holiday Inns, KFC, Dairy Queen, Domino's Pizza, Jamba Juice, Mathnasium, Subway, Visiting Angels, and Wendy's would never have succeeded in reaching national or global markets.

Kroc saw his success and that of his franchisees as a co-dependent outcome. "My belief was that I had to help the individual operator succeed in every way I could. His success would ensure my success." Kroc encouraged his operators to be innovative. A McDonald's franchisee in Washington sponsored a local television show that developed the character of Ronald McDonald. A Pittsburgh operator, experimenting with how to satisfy customers looking for bigger hamburgers, created the Big Mac. The

Filet-O-Fish was invented by a Cincinnati owner in the 1960s for Catholic customers who, before Church rules changed, didn't eat meat on Fridays.

## Successful Franchises

Success among the franchisees of already strong brands is more likely for a variety of reasons. Entrepreneurs who become franchisees—generally called "operators" in the franchise world—are older and more experienced than other entrepreneurs. The average age of a franchise buyer is forty-six; only about ten percent of new operators are under thirty-five, and nearly ten percent are over sixty-five. Overwhelmingly, franchise buyers have significant employment or business histories, and most have built up savings and other assets.

To purchase a strong brand, however, having sufficient financial means is not enough. Most established franchisors screen applicants very carefully; in addition to in-depth and detailed financial background checks, their due diligence may include interviews with friends, neighbors, and family members, and some require that applicants undergo psychological testing. Obviously, these franchisors need to feel confident about an applicant's level of commitment and fit within their business model, and to know whether the applicant will be a worthy representative of the brand that the franchisor works so hard to maintain and improve. Successful franchising companies pride themselves on their careful selection processes and how successful their operators become.

Long-established franchisors work hard to perfect and innovate their product and service offerings and their business formulas. For example, every franchisor specifies, often with excruciating particularity, the size and appearance of the brand's building. With very few exceptions, and no exceptions within the top two hundred franchisors in the U.S., those companies supply assistance to an operator in negotiating for location and with building contractors, require often intensive initial and ongoing training for franchisees and their managers and supervisors, and strictly control supply chains for everything from equipment to the size of napkins or the design of the dining room chairs. To ensure that a Big Mac tastes the same in Seattle and Savannah, McDonald's operators and their key employees are required to attend "Hamburger U," and must purchase their "Special Sauce" from an approved supplier.

A number of successful franchise operations reflect their founders' intentional creation of business models that can be successfully and uniformly replicated. Snap-On Tools, Panera Bread, Aaron Rents, Servpro, and 7-Eleven began this way. Richard Melman started his first restaurant when he was twenty-nine. In the next twenty years, he opened ten more. In 1991, he decided that he wanted to build a restaurant that, if successful, could become a franchise model. He experimented with an old-fashioned bakery–coffee shop in downtown Chicago's business district. Today, there are two hundred Corner Bakery locations, many in busy airports.

Much like Melman, Phil Romano started a dozen single-location restaurants after college. It wasn't until he was forty that he hit upon the idea of Fuddruckers, now a national chain featuring premium hamburgers, and then went on to create Romano's Macaroni Grill, a two hundred location franchise. Romano told me that he believes his real talent is sensing customer trends, what people will want next. "Because the restaurant market is so dynamic, you have to be anticipating changing consumer tastes." In 2014, Romano created an experimental all-restaurant mall in suburban Dallas, where he invites aspiring entrepreneurs to test their concepts as potential franchises that he might develop.

## How Do You Decide If a Franchise Is Your Right First Business?

Perhaps, like Bob Carlucci, you aren't so sure that you can devise an innovation good enough to become a great company. So, as a first step into the entrepreneurial world, you decide to consider a franchised business, becoming an operator for an existing brand. How should you go about finding the right opportunity?

The first part of an answer to that question lies in picking an industry in which you have some interest and perhaps even some experience. If you aren't much interested in how food is made, maybe a gym, rather than a Burger King, is the right answer. Having an interest in cars may point to a Jiffy Lube. A talent for working with kids might lead an aspiring franchisee to an enriched curriculum childcare business like Goddard School, or a franchised tutoring and learning service.

Once personal interest and experience have narrowed the field, a potential franchisee should look at the widest possible array of opportunities. That research begins with a combination of assessing your financial capacity to purchase a particular franchise and getting the materials that every company will supply. For example, an existing McDonald's location is pricey: according to the company, it can require a total investment of one to more than two million dollars, including liquid capital of $750,000 and a franchise fee of $45,000. Other franchise opportunities, even those with established brands and good reputations, may be much less costly.

You also will need to examine—with help from an experienced lawyer—the "franchise agreement," the contract that will control the relationship between the franchisor and the franchisee. Understanding and analyzing that agreement is critical to any applicant's decision; it likely will bind you to the franchisor for ten to twenty years and, for a franchisee, "divorce" can be a painful and expensive process. Almost all states require franchisors to be licensed before offering franchises for sale, which means that they have submitted their standard agreements for a regulator's review. And, similar to the government's oversight of the sale of a publicly traded company's stock, both state and federal laws require that a franchisee agreement disclose all of the important terms and conditions of the relationship. Nonetheless, franchise agreements are complicated documents, and it's important that you understand what you're buying. One of the most critical elements of the franchise agreement is the definition of a franchisee's rights to an exclusive geographic area, a "territory," in which the franchisee has the sole right to develop additional locations and, even more important, precludes other locations of the same franchise moving in to compete nearby. Turning to an experienced franchisee lawyer is critical.

As a potential franchisee, you will need to research and explore opportunities while being very mindful that franchisors are trying to recruit qualified applicants. The sales pitch to an attractive candidate likely will be bullish and persuasive. After all, the business of the corporate parent is not to fry hamburgers or supervise home health care aides, it's to make franchises. Be skeptical and well-prepared for these conversations and don't be hurried into a decision. Aspiring franchisee-entrepreneurs often take three or four years to decide on an opportunity that best suits their talents, ambitions, expectations, and price range.

As you compare opportunities, imagine yourself owning that operation and working there every day. That brand will become your brand. Are you comfortable with the franchisor's products and services, its values, its business methods, and the franchise agreement that you'll sign? Your decision should be shaped by the answers that you receive to six questions.

### Is the Market Niche Stable?

Every business exists to fulfill or create a market need. Obviously, franchising focuses on the "fulfill" side of business as the franchise product or service is (or should be), by definition, a proven concept. But markets are dynamic, determined by consumer preferences, changing technology, and economic conditions. Before Netflix gave us mail-order DVD delivery (their first-stage ancient history) and today's streaming video, there were nearly nine thousand Blockbuster stores across America that rented DVDs to walk-in customers. You wouldn't have wanted to buy the last franchise sold. Likewise, Sbarro was once a coveted brand with a targeted market of teenage mall rats, a population that disappeared when social media enabled more spontaneous meet-ups in many other places.

When evaluating a franchise opportunity, it's also important to acknowledge that changing economic conditions influence some businesses more than others. Recessions are tough on lawn-care businesses but great for car-repair franchises. Pizza and dog grooming seem immune to economic fluctuations. Specialty food franchises, including those that sell cookies, gelato, and boutique cupcakes, flourish until consumer tastes move on.

### What Do Other Franchisees Say?

As soon as you're focused on one or even two franchises as a possibility, begin talking to its current operators. Most franchisees will be forthcoming about nearly everything, including profits. (After all, you won't be locating in their "territory"; you'll be a colleague, not a competitor.) Ask if their experience mirrors the franchisor's portrayal of the investment needed for the franchise, and the projected sales and expected profits. If there are differences, how does the franchisee explain them? Have they received the expected or needed support from the franchisor? Does their parent's reputation affect their sales, either positively or negatively? What is their experience with the franchisor's commitment to marketing and advertising? Does it square with the promises that were made? Ask how the franchisee would describe her ongoing relationship with the brand and "corporate": Is it easy to get assistance from the home office when it's needed? Does the franchisor help to solve problems? Are required supply chains well managed? Are the products of good quality?

### How Do I Make Money, and How Much?

Unlike entrepreneurs choosing other paths, buying a franchise provides the best chance to analyze the investment before setting forth on the journey. Existing operating units, often called "stores," provide tangible examples of the business in real time. Can you discern how profit is made, and how to make more?

A franchise should be tested as an investment. Will the return on capital invested, plus the time and pressures of running this new business, pay off? As a general rule, a franchise should return at least fifteen percent profit every year after the first three years. Will your yield, after three years, be at least as much as if your money had been conservatively invested and you had continued to work regular hours at a regular job?

There are a number of elements critical to a franchisee's analysis of the future value of a franchise investment. As mentioned earlier, the terms of the agreement between the corporate franchisor and the franchisee is key, and this is most particularly true with respect to the franchisor's grant to a franchisee of exclusivity in a defined "territory." You don't want your hard work and investment jeopardized by a new franchisee's location just around the corner. Reputable franchisors value their brands and their relationships with their operators, which is how they make their profitable businesses grow and thrive; they don't usually engage in undercutting.

But, look carefully at a franchisor's record on this front—it is a common source of friction between franchisees and franchisors—and be mindful that this is a very important term of your agreement, especially with less-established franchisors.

## How Will the Brand Support You?

Strong franchises provide education and continual training about how to be a successful operator, usually in the form of an ongoing and valuable curriculum. In established and successful franchising companies, attending training school is a required step. Does the franchisor that you're considering provide effective training? Beyond learning how to run the store, are there programs to help you increase sales and improve profitability?

Successful franchise companies also know that location is key to success and that they need to provide direction and assistance on this front. For fast food, childcare, or a walk-in critical-care facility, siting in a well-traversed, and easily noticed and located, area is critical. A carpet-cleaning franchise can locate in a back-street warehouse district; that business usually goes to its customers, not the other way around. The next time that you pass through an airport, notice where the best franchises are located. Auntie Anne's, devised to be a quick and portable snack before or during a flight, often is found at the intersection of two piers, the highest-trafficked spots in airports. Frequently, established franchisors offer already-determined locations and building sites for sale when they know that they want to expand into new areas.

Financing is another area in which franchisors generally will aid and support new franchisees and established franchisees who seek to expand. All reputable franchisors require franchisee applicants to show that they have sufficient funds or assets—or the creditworthiness to borrow—to buy or lease real estate and build and equip the store, and also have sufficient financial resources to cover operating losses in the first year of operation. Many franchisors provide direct financing. Chick-fil-A, which is known for its meticulously careful selection of franchisees, then commits to those operators and will provide most of the startup capital needed to buy land and build stores. But, be inquisitive and prudent on this front: Depending on your financial situation and experience, you may be able to secure better financing terms from an independent lender than from your franchisor.

### What Is the Franchisor's Record of Innovation?

One of the secrets of great franchisors is that they stay ahead of market trends and keep their brands relevant and responsive to consumer preferences. To thrive and grow, they must balance brand discipline with sufficient innovation to ensure growing market share and to continuously improve their operators' incomes.

McDonald's, for example, constantly tests and modifies its menu to reflect even subtle changes in customer demand. "All Day Breakfast" was one such shift that has become a real success. Obviously, it is much more difficult for franchises built around a single product or service to introduce new selections as consumer preferences wax and wane. A Beanie Baby franchise network would not have prospered.

### Who Will Give Me Expert Advice?

A number of established franchisors enjoy very positive reputations for their support of their operators and the success that those franchisees have had. Not all franchisors, however, are as committed or honest. Every year, we see hundreds of ideas that proclaim that they are "the new McDonald's" of small-job printing, pest control, gutter replacement, or home repair services. More than 3,500 franchise opportunities now exist in the U.S., and that number probably grows every day. Sometimes, unscrupulous "entreprepreneur"-hustlers attempt to franchise ideas that have never been successful as a business in even a single location. Notwithstanding the government oversight in place to protect potential buyers, offers may come wrapped in unsubstantiated promises and invented statistics. Being among the first franchisees of any unproven business concept is a risky choice.

If you choose to be a franchisee-entrepreneur, do your research, consider only licensed franchisors, spend time with an experienced franchise lawyer, and talk to a knowledgeable loan officer at the bank. Every hour that you spend to understand what you're getting into will improve the decision that you make and enhance the chances of your success.

# CHAPTER 8

# Preventing Failure
# Before It Happens

Again and again, aspiring entrepreneurs hear and read that failure is our most important teacher. That advice always rings hollow. It sounds as if the very tangible and painful costs of a business failure, only partly measured in a damaged career and lost savings, can be excused or breezily wished away by saying the entrepreneur must have learned a lot.

No one starts a business to have a learning experience. Very few business or self-help books, and yet fewer on entrepreneurship, celebrate failure. Those that do offer fluffy advice, like "Fail forward" or "Fail fast."

Nor is evidence supportive of the thesis that entrepreneurs find failure a great teacher. There are exceptions to every rule, of course: Bill Gates and Paul Allen crashed their first company, Traf-O-Data, before starting Microsoft; Milton Hershey failed three times before he succeeded in the candy bar business; and Walt Disney's first company, Laugh-O-Grams, went bankrupt.

But, for most entrepreneurs—more than two-thirds—failing at

one business means that they will never try again. Perhaps that's a sensible idea, as the chances of success are no better for those who try a second time. If failure is a source of insight, it should teach lessons that aspiring entrepreneurs can use to increase their chances of starting successful companies.

Simply put, startups are different one from the other, so the reasons for their failures are different. As the following stories illustrate, failure comes in all shapes and sizes, and it fells not only—although most commonly—the novice entrepreneur but also the seasoned and experienced. What seemed to work for one new venture may be the wrong direction for another. A better approach is to internalize the generic risks that all new companies face. Thus equipped, you may be able to steer clear of minefields and minimize your chances of failure.

## Taking Sixteen Years to Fail

Even as a boy, Nick Franano saw himself as a doctor, helping people. After college, he studied medicine at Washington University and did his residency and a research fellowship at Johns Hopkins. Like most young researchers at Hopkins, Franano seemed destined to be a professor of medicine, someday having his own laboratory and teaching some of the world's most promising medical students.

One patient's predicament, however, turned Franano into an entrepreneur. He was specializing in kidney diseases, and most of his Hopkins patients would eventually need dialysis. The dialysis procedure requires that a patient be hooked up to a machine every three or four days to have her blood filtered and returned to her body. Without dialysis, impurities in the patient's blood will poison her, leading to rather rapid death. Without a kidney transplant, she likely will spend time in and out of dialysis clinics several times a week for the remainder of her life.

Before dialysis can begin, every patient must undergo a surgical procedure by which a site on her body is prepared for the insertion of catheters that will permit access to the circulatory system. These catheters allow the patient's blood to pass from the body into the dialysis machine, where it is filtered, and back into the body. Once in place, inserted catheters need continuous maintenance and present myriad potential problems.

One of Franano's patients was having particular trouble with his catheter insertion site, and ended up at the hospital six times in two weeks because his veins were collapsing around it. Each visit involved a minor but painful surgery to move the site of the catheter insertions to another spot on his body. In the midst of one such visit, the exasperated patient asked Franano why no one had found a way for blood vessels to fix themselves.

That simple question triggered Franano's imagination and his search for an answer. He knew that the dialysis process gradually caused blood vessels to lose their elasticity and begin to harden because the middle layer, which delivers nourishment to the tough outer and inner layers, itself begins to harden and then slowly die. As this occurs, arteries and veins around the catheter insertion site start to collapse, which requires that the insertion site be relocated. The ultimate risk is that, after years of dialysis, a patient may run out of places on his body that are able to host the catheter.

Franano's research took him to an untested formula, PRT-201, a compound that he theorized might rejuvenate and strengthen the middle layers of the veins and arteries. He experimented by setting up two groups of pigs and inserting catheters into each, then injecting the PRT-201 into the surrounding veins and arteries of one group. In the pigs without PRT-201 injections, the veins and arteries collapsed much like those in humans, becoming hard, inflexible, and necrotic around the ports. The veins and arteries of pigs injected with PRT-201 seemed to remain flexible and soft for many months longer. It took three more years to reproduce and confirm his lab studies in successively larger groups of pigs, and the invention of a special needle to inject PRT-201 into the middle layers of vessels, before Franano could try experimenting with human patients.

Armed with laboratory data showing the effectiveness of PRT-201 in pigs, and with his newly developed delivery mechanism, Franano approached several drug companies, expecting that one would want to license his discovery. He soon learned, however, that early stage experimental drugs are seldom of interest to big pharmaceutical manufacturers. The necessary double-blind human trials were very costly, they said, and there were too few dialysis patients to make a new drug economically feasible. Knowing how badly dialysis patients needed help, Franano took the gigantic step of starting a new company, Proteon Therapeutics, to commercialize his experimental drug.

His first task was to convince a small group of investors to back him. In 2005, they provided $2 million to fund his company's test of PRT-201 with a small group of dialysis patients. After three years, positive clinical results allowed Proteon to raise an additional $15 million from two venture capital funds. With this money, Franano started the next round of clinical trials necessary to convince the federal Food and Drug Administration (FDA) of the drug's efficacy and its safety.

After seven years, preliminary results from the second trial again looked positive. To investors, Proteon looked like it had a promising future. If its drug, now bearing a trade name, Vonapanitase, was judged to be effective in helping dialysis patients live longer, and could be used to help a much larger population suffering from peripheral artery disease, as Franano had begun to suspect over the course of his research, the company would own what in the pharmaceutical industry is referred to as a "blockbuster drug."

Now, other investors were eager to line up behind Proteon. Relying on Franano's clinical data, the investors added another $92 million in venture funding. With such a vote of confidence, the company raised an additional $72 million when it sold stock in a public offering in October 2014.

Immediately, the company began the FDA's Phase III clinical trials for Vonapanitase, recruiting hundreds of dialysis patients in thirty-one medical centers for a double-blind clinical study. Because earlier studies, with smaller numbers of patients, had shown substantial positive effects, Franano and his investors had reason to believe that they had a winner. Over time, the stock climbed from its IPO price of $11 to over $20 per share, with financial analysts suggesting that, as soon as the new clinical data was in hand, the stock would double in price. "Easily a forty-dollar stock," said one.

After two years of following large numbers of both treated patients and a control group, independent researchers participating in the Phase III FDA trial found no statistical evidence of the drug's efficacy, the FDA standard for market approval.[1] When news of the trial's failure became public, the company's stock price cratered to $2 per share, the equivalent value of its cash on hand.

Franano had worked on his new drug for sixteen years. He had written three business plans and raised $181 million in capital from venture and public investors. Up until the very last minute, he believed that he could give kidney-disease patients a solution that would extend their lives and reduce their pain. Franano believed that he was at the vanguard of hope for those patients and, perhaps, for other patients suffering other types of circulatory disease. While the FDA's drug approval process is famously complex and unpredictable, Franano's investors were experienced and knowledgeable about the risks of investing in a new drug. But, in the world of startups, the past is not always prologue.

## From the White House to Malls

Dean Kamen is an inventor genius, widely regarded as the Thomas Edison of our time. His innovative talent is legendary; working in his private laboratory, he has patented over four hundred inventions. His creative streak prompted him to drop out of college in the early 1970s to create a wearable infusion pump, now an inseparable part of life for many diabetics who depend on insulin therapy. Among many other innovative devices, he subsequently invented a coronary stent, an implantable device that has saved the lives of many stroke victims, and the iBot, a remarkable all-terrain wheelchair that can climb stairs. Kamen developed the iBot for the Defense Department to help paraplegic veterans become more mobile.

In the late 1990s, Kamen began work on what he termed a "personal transporter," a new kind of individual mobility device. He worked in secret, fearing that, if word got out, others would copy it. Historically, Kamen had patented his inventions and licensed them to companies that would manufacture them, but this time, he planned to build a company around his revolutionary device. Kamen's spectacular track record made it possible for him to raise $90 million in venture funding without a business plan, as he refused to commit his idea to paper. His investors were sworn to secrecy about his concept.[2]

Through the summer of 2001, in anticipation of the unveiling of a new Kamen invention, hype began to build. The outside world knew only that Kamen was up to something big and that it was code-named "Ginger." Kamen would say only that Ginger would revolutionize transportation and would be "to the car what the car was to the horse and buggy." Excitement grew when Steve Jobs, who had seen a top-secret prototype, said Kamen's invention would be as big as the PC. John Doerr, perhaps the most influential venture investor in Silicon Valley, declared it would be more important than the Internet.

On December 3, 2001, Kamen unveiled the Segway. A brilliant combination of computers, gyroscopes, batteries, sensors, and small electric motors, it was compared by one reporter to the reinvention of the wheel. Athletes, movie stars, and President Bush—at the White House—were filmed gleefully riding the elegant device. Kamen predicted that his invention would displace cars and buses on city streets, refashioning an old philosopher's adage to declare, "The city needs a car like a fish needs a bicycle." Jeff Bezos, founder of Amazon agreed, saying, "Cities will be built around this device." He saw people commuting to work on Segways, eliminating traffic.

Within weeks after models were released for sale, it became clear there was no market demand for this ingenious product. Fifteen years later, the Segway's users mostly are security guards inside shopping malls and airports. Despite being a technical tour de force, the public didn't care. Kamen's dream was to manufacture millions of personal transporters every year. Today's annual worldwide sales total about six thousand.

When I asked Kamen why the Segway had flopped, he blamed himself for misjudging the trajectory of technology and jumping too far ahead. "It was a rookie mistake. I tried to invent what I thought people really needed, not the next thing they might really use." He went on with a chagrined smile, "I knew I'd made a mistake when, after being astonished by the Segway, the first question people usually asked was, 'What do you do when it rains?' " Kamen found it hard to believe that city planners didn't embrace the Segway; he saw it as their chance to wipe out street traffic and eliminate the need for parking garages. Instead, all they talked about was how crowded and dangerous sidewalks would become. When I first watched a Segway video clip with my wife, a busy urban professional, she rolled her eyes and remarked, "Where do I put the kids' car seats and the groceries?" Kamen's humbling experience certainly reminded him—and should be front and center for every innovator–entrepreneur—of the need to realistically assess potential market demand. Even a wildly successful inventor genius can get things wrong.

After the Segway flop, Kamen returned to his lab, where he continues to create. In 2010, he unveiled a marvelous autonomous prosthetic arm. "Luke" attaches to nerves that once controlled the user's original limb, and the arm intuitively responds to brain commands.

## Sailing into Failure

A sailing-enthusiast engineering student—I'll call him Tony Seaman for the painful part of his story—was transformed into an entrepreneur before he left college. Going into his senior year, he was looking for an easy elective. Knowing nothing except that other engineering students had said that "Introduction to Entrepreneurship" was a piece of cake, he signed up. Some of his engineering professors had started companies and he knew that many engineers became entrepreneurs. So, he thought, it might be helpful to know how the process worked.

Tony later described the experience to me: "Besides listening to a professor stretch a few hours of actual information into four months of lectures," all that was required of students was writing a business plan. As in thousands of similar courses offered each year, he had two weeks to propose an idea for a business. The principal guidance the professor offered was to look to a personal passion for inspiration. To Tony, that meant sailing. He had grown up just a mile from the Atlantic, and had worked in a boatyard every summer since he was fourteen.

Tony's business plan described a solution to a problem that he thought he might encounter the following year when he would be living in New York City, surrounded by water without anywhere near enough money to keep a sailboat in a marina. He envisioned a folding catamaran that would weigh fewer than one hundred pounds, fit in a travel bag, and could be carried on the subway and stored in a closet. Tony had taken a course in materials sciences, so he knew that he could make his hypothetical boat with strong lightweight carbon fiber.

Two weeks later, when it was his turn to describe his idea in class, Tony made a simple origami-like folding paper model. He followed his professor's prompt, hyping his idea when pitching it to the class. "This is not some flimsy portable boat, but one with serious performance capabilities, not a Toyota but an Aston Martin." When he finished, his professor excitedly declared, "You have got to make this into a real company." After winning his university's business-plan competition, Tony was a star on campus, celebrated as if he already was a successful entrepreneur.

Warming to the idea of his catamaran, and encouraged by his professors and the enthusiasm of the competition judges, Tony turned down job offers from engineering firms. Instead he moved to New York, took a part-time job as a bartender, and began to work on his boat. Unfortunately, his enthusiasm outweighed his grasp of several pertinent facts. Among them was that sailboat sales had been in a steep decline for over a decade, with only one-fifth as many being sold in 2014 as in 2004; apparently, sailboarding and kite-surfing had made huge dents in the market.

Further, using the materials required to make a boat light enough to carry resulted in its costing at least $24,000. With no customers in sight but already a self-declared entrepreneur, Tony attempted to make his boat so revolutionary that it had to sell. He designed new rudders with embedded gyroscopes, so that a first-time user could sail like a professional. His blueprints described the world's first self-driving sailboat, but to build it would have added another ten thousand dollars to the cost of each boat.

When I asked Tony how he came to believe that anyone would spend $34,000 for his folding sailboat when they could rent a sailboat at a marina many times over for the same price, he argued that Elon Musk's strategy had been to sell his first cars to wealthy customers as a means to finance more affordable models for subsequent sales to a wider audience. I reminded him that Musk had customers begging for cars just on the rumors that it was being built. People wanted a cool electric car regardless of price. Did he ever have any evidence there was any such latent demand for a folding boat?

Tony was continuously cheered on by those around him who defaulted to encouragement and support when they might better have played devil's advocate. They were his "hot circle." I was the only one throwing cold water on his idea, refusing his entreaties to invest and explaining that a market for his idea would never materialize.

After banging his head against a wall for two years, Tony decided to give up and to enter a master's program in engineering at Berkeley, planning to concentrate in robotics and autonomous sensor control systems. Before returning to school, however, he needed to save some money and took a job in a marine engineering firm. It was there that Tony discovered that ocean-going freighters were not coordinating their data streams to optimize fuel consumption. This was nearly incomprehensible to him: How could vessels that cost hundreds of millions of dollars and carried many multiples of their value in cargo with each load have no artificial intelligence on board like cars and trucks do? In ships, such devices could help determine the most efficient speed and fuel use for changing weather and ocean conditions and continuously adjust routing. Tony began a period of intensive research and discovered a hole in the technology support of a giant industry, a critical part of the logistics network that makes global commerce possible.

"Tony"—who for the happy part of his story is really Anthony DiMare—is a member of the small club of failed entrepreneurs who decided to take another turn at bat. This time around, he has had the good fortune to have developed a network of really accomplished advisers. (Many aspiring entrepreneurs waste time networking with what might be called "poseur" experts, people—often failed entrepreneurs—who project an image of possessing knowledge and experience that they really don't.) Fortunately, DiMare's new network included Bre Pettis, one of the founders of Maker-Bot. A great network involves important secondary connections, and Pettis, once he was convinced about the potential of DiMare's technology and vision, opened doors. In 2016, Nautilus Labs was created with $2 million in venture funding and, even more important, a letter of intent to buy its navigational assistance intelligence system for a fleet of twenty-two vessels. DiMare started Nautilus Labs without a business plan.

When I asked DiMare if he had learned anything from his first company that he thinks will improve his chance for success in Nautilus Labs, he considered the question carefully. His reply was interesting. "Nothing that I shouldn't have known before I wrote my first business plan. Bad ideas can't lead to good companies. The smartest thing I did was to break it off. I worried, though, that if I went back to school, I'd never have a chance to start a company again. So I put Berkeley on hold. Maybe what I learned is to have a plan if my next startup fails—but it won't. I hope what

I've learned is a kind of smart determination, the importance of research and how to quickly size up people who can really help me and tell them apart from those who can't."

## No One Knows Why Startups Fail

The stories of Franano, Kamen, and DiMare are unsettling. No one wants to think about starting a company that will fall flat. Statistics remind us, however, that success is the exception for startups: The norm is failure. What can you do to avoid it?

A casual search of the Internet will provide dozens of alleged most important causes of startup failure. Many are plausible, but most won't be helpful to understanding how you can avoid them in your new company. These are called *point risks*, so named because they identify specific points of failure, many of which have been self-identified by the founders of failed ventures.

Perhaps the most oft-cited reason for failure is that a company couldn't get to the other side of what is widely referred to as the Valley of Death, the period after its founding where a company can't raise enough money to finish developing its product. It dies from lack of resources well before it can reach the point where its cup runneth over.

The reason that the Valley of Death looms so large as the putative cause of startup failure is that virtually every unsuccessful entrepreneur believes that he would have been successful if only he had had more time, which translates to more money and more faithful investors. "If only" is the most credible, most easily defended, and least blame-worthy excuse.

But startups rarely ever fail for just one reason. H. L. Mencken's famous quip applies: "For every complex problem there is an answer that is clear, simple, and wrong." Knowing that many unsuccessful entrepreneurs believe that they failed because they ran out of money is not particularly helpful and, in most cases, it is likely just wrong. Besides, is the conclusion that you should, above all else, stop working on your business and focus on raising more money? How does that vicious cycle end?

Money surely wasn't Franano's problem. From the start, he had the backing of both sophisticated seed and seasoned venture capital firms for a very promising new drug. Their infusion of $109 million, an amount many times greater than the average venture-backed firm ever receives, encouraged public shareholders, many of whom were knowledgeable biotech investors, to provide millions more. Similarly, Kamen's Segway didn't fail for want of capital. His reputation garnered him the generous backing of some of the most successful investors in Silicon Valley. And, even if "Tony" had been able to raise money from family and friends, what would've happened when he couldn't sell enough folding sailboats to continue production, much less return investors' capital?

Another frequently mentioned cause of failure, conflict among the company's founders, didn't explain these failures either. Each was the leader of a pack of one. With no co-founders, they didn't face internal conflict. Similarly, cautions about taking a product to market prematurely can't explain the failure of any of these companies. The FDA controlled if and when Franano's drug could be marketed. Had it worked, every dialysis patient would have believed that it was long overdue. Kamen's product, however, was unlikely to have been any more successful in 2010 than it was in 2001.

In addition to collapsing in the Valley of Death, companies frequently are said to fail because they did not compete competently against others supplying similar products. "Tony" was not outdone by a better folding sailboat any more than Franano or Kamen were beaten by better products or more effective marketing campaigns. They promised one-of-a-kind products, so that wasn't the problem.

The dedication of Franano, Kamen, and "Tony" to the success

of their inventions was unswerving, so distracted entrepreneur syndrome also didn't apply, either. That's the name for another frequently cited cause for startup failures—that the entrepreneur is really a hobby jobber who is not fully committed to his project, or someone who has aspirations and initiative but is unable or unwilling to leave a secure full-time job to devote the necessary time to his new efforts.

The problem of analyzing startup failure with notional lists of reasons for startup failures is a snake biting its tail; a too-well-schooled entrepreneur may begin to see success as the product of cautiously steering his venture around potential land mines. The job of the entrepreneur from this perspective becomes one of not making mistakes, of keeping her company from failing. While every entrepreneur faces the task of nurturing her idea, focusing on failure avoidance is not a winning strategy.

## Insure Your Own Startup

All startups face generic risks. Knowing this suggests a better way to improve your startup's odds of success: Don't focus on the specific risks, but anticipate the generic risks and attempt to mitigate or minimize their impact ahead of time.

The distinction between specific and generic risks becomes clear if you apply an insurance analogy—perhaps a rather dry subject for many of us. But we all understand that, in essence, an insurance company is in the business of risk assessment. Think about buying a fire-insurance policy on your startup's factory. The insurance company will set the availability, coverage, and price of a policy based on its experience of the likely risk of having to pay a claim. Fire insurance will pay off if your factory is damaged or burned to the ground. So, the first thing that the insurance company will do is gather information to assess the risk of fire. Is the factory making dynamite or shoes? Is it built of wood or brick? Does it have smoke detectors and a sprinkler system? How far is it from the closest firehouse? Your insurer also will consider whether you have taken certain steps to prevent fire in the first place, for example, segregated used flammable materials appropriately and fire-retardant carpeting and ceiling tiles. The insurance company will require you to become a partner in minimizing the risk of fire.

Work from this analogy to think about your startup in terms of a loss from which you might never recover. What generic risks can you identify and manage so that, from the very first moment, you can increase the chances of ultimate success? What can you do to mitigate the chances of failure? An aspiring entrepreneur should make the same ruthless assessment of the value of his idea as would an insurance company—as if you could buy "failure insurance." It is, after all, your investment: your time, your effort, and your money, both in absolute terms and in terms of foregone or bypassed alternate pursuits.

## Research Research Research

There is no recovering from an idea that just cannot become a successful business. As we have seen in most of the stories in this book, no startup is certain that there is a market for the innovation it wants to develop. Some ideas, however, are inherently more likely to fail.

Such ideas seem to occupy wannapreneurs, those who go looking for an idea but whose real intent is just to start a company, more than other aspiring entrepreneurs. Had Anthony been more skeptical about the chances of his sailboat appealing to customers, he might have saved himself the three years that he attempted to make a product that no one would likely buy. He might have mitigated his risk, played at being his own insurance company, by doing some critical research.

Unfortunately, there is something about the excitement of conceiving what feels like a great idea that can cause many would-be entrepreneurs to resist having their vision disturbed, no matter what. With a little searching, Anthony could have discovered the major fall-off in sailboat sales, and that the carbon fiber material that he needed would make his boat prohibitively expensive to sell. Perhaps, if he'd been equipped with that information, he might have decided to abandon that idea and search for something more feasible. Or, if a better idea didn't come to him at that moment, he might have taken a job in an engineering firm and had that better idea a few years later.

Ironically, an aversion to research is most pronounced among college students, the most computer-savvy generation on earth. For them, being able to study the trajectory of technology should be easier than for other entrepreneurs without their access to a university's special resources. For example, professors with specific expertise generally are just a few buildings away. Yet, time after time, when judging business plan competitions, the apparent absence of critical background knowledge has caused me to ask, "Have you tested the feasibility of making this?" Or, "Have you examined patent filings to see what related inventions might already exist?"[3] Or, "Hasn't someone already tried to convert a similar idea into a product?" Before Anthony entered the business-plan competition, shouldn't his professor–sponsor have asked if he had done any informal market research outside of his own hot circle of friends? Did Anthony ever ask anyone who wasn't a friend or a family member or who otherwise wasn't rooting for his success if they would want a folding sailboat enough to pay $34,000 for it?

The problem of not doing sufficient practical research to prevent a disaster is not limited to college students, as the story of Kamen's Segway tells. Kamen was captured by the vision of his personal transporter. Given his track record, he raised money immediately. Given his reputation, what investor would not want to be part of the first big Kamen company? They all likely worried that, if they passed, Kamen would go on to other investors and then they'd end up feeling like all of us who didn't buy Amazon at twenty-six dollars in 2006.

A little research might have revealed that market demand really couldn't exist. Imagine if Kamen had previewed his idea with even a handful of potential customers. First, he likely would have recognized a prosaic competitor hiding in plain sight, the lightweight motorcycle. These versatile machines are valued by urban commuters around the world for their speed, agility in traffic, ease of parking and storage, and fuel economy. Small motorcycles have never been widely adopted in the United States, however, because our average commutes are much longer and the severe weather in many parts of the country limits their utility. Even if the Segway eventually could have replaced the lightweight motorcycle on the basis of cost, it was not as practical; there was no room for the plastic-encased baby carrier or the crate for purchases that one sees on the backs of motorbikes on rainy days in Paris or Jakarta.

## Avoid Technology Traps

Investors sometimes do more research on a proposed business than the entrepreneur ever did. What? How can that be possible? I was totally flummoxed when I encountered this for the first time, and thought that I should rub my eyes to dispel the mirage. Investors not only are trying to assess the potential of a business idea for growth, the idiom of all venture investors, but, just as important, they are assessing their risk, trying to see what could go wrong. What are they looking for?

By their very nature, startups exist to bring new ideas to the market. In their quest for unique products, however, many entrepreneurs fall into what might be called the "technology trap." Because technology *permits* something new to be accomplished, the entrepreneur presumes that a need for that something new will emerge. This often appears to be the "logic of invention." The cell phone comes to mind. We didn't know we needed it until it appeared.

But, the logic of invention is not absolute. Many inventions appear for which there is no need at all. Thousands of products that are invented every year solve problems that don't really exist. No one needed the patented device to hard boil eggs into squares so they would be easier to slice, or a cell phone with the built-in razor.

The Internet of Everything, an historic point in the evolution of digital technology, allows for new syntheses where smart devices communicate with one another, thus permitting new products to emerge. Those products reveal latent needs that didn't become clear until a solution appeared, one that was dependent on devices communicating among themselves. Anyone who has lost a dog thanks his lucky stars that Max is wearing a GPS collar that can pinpoint him in seconds. Millions of people now remotely monitor their home's security and energy use from halfway around the world. Amazon has taken us one step closer to merely speaking to make things happen; instead of rummaging through the CD drawer, I ask Alexa for my favorite album. Google's Home will do the same if you say, "Hey, Google, get me . . ."

Other applications are interesting but without much value. FlightRadar24 can tell you that the shining speck five miles overhead is Delta's flight 234 from Frankfurt to Atlanta. That's fun to know on a clear starry night at the beach, but, practically speaking, it's mostly useless information. Some so-called discoveries are actually counterproductive. As a business plan competition judge I have encountered smart frying pans on three different campuses. By building sensors into a pan, the would-be entrepreneurs then designed cell-phone apps that tell the user when his eggs are ready. Never has frying an egg been so complicated. Just because it can be made doesn't mean it's likely to be useful.

Investors try very hard to assess the actual utility and marketability of proposed products and services in deciding if they'll make a bet. Aspiring entrepreneurs should do likewise. "New" is not enough. Not everything is the Internet, or even a better vacuum cleaner.

## Beware Regulatory Trip Wires

Proteon was felled by the regulatory process at the FDA. Like it or not—and a lot of critics make a credible case that the process is deeply flawed—Franano and all of his investors, both private and public, knew the rules and set out, at considerable expense, to run the marathon.

Other kinds of regulatory risks, much less likely to be foreseen from the outset, also can bring down a new venture. Today, if a neighbor got a whiff of the toxic fumes that Howard Head was cooking up in his unventilated garage workshop, Head likely would be shut down and probably fined. These kinds of risks—zoning violations for manufacturing in the wrong area, improper disposal of waste from your production process, failure to properly calculate payroll taxes, even a neighbor reporting that there are too many cars parked outside your house or too many courier trucks pulling up in your residential neighborhood—can stop a new and thinly financed startup dead in its tracks, or at least distract the entrepreneur while he cleans up a bureaucratic mess.

Not all regulatory agency rules are easily ascertainable, but startup founders should stop for a few minutes to consider what might apply, then do some basic research to see what they can do to minimize these risks. Federal, state, and even municipal employment rules get more complicated as a business scales up and brings on more workers, and the ability of agencies to shut down businesses and freeze or even seize bank accounts is very real. Not that every startup needs a fancy corporate lawyer to assess which rules might apply, but it's a good idea to do some basic work on this front.

There's an intersection between regulatory traps and the need to do research. Just a few years ago, two student wannapreneurs came to see me about their great idea, complete with diagrams, spread sheets, and enthusiasm about the improved health outcomes that would result from their startup. They wanted to set up an auction exchange entity that would match buyers and sellers of human organs, which they asserted would make the matching process much more efficient and transparent than the current registry system and would thus save the lives of more people in desperate need of replacement organs. They thought that any negative perception that the exchange would favor wealthy persons could be dissipated by crowd funding or by insurance companies purchasing organs for their insureds. Their exchange would make money through fees paid by buyers and also take a piece of the spread between the bid and the ask, like the financial market makers in the old days. I listened for a patient five minutes before I interrupted, "Have you checked the federal laws about the purchase of human organs?" I turned in my chair and typed the term into my computer, and the answer was definitive in about ten seconds. The business they proposed was illegal. They were dumbstruck.

## Keep Your Vision Flexible

You can control risk by making sure that your company remains open to opportunity in its earliest days. There is an old Southern expression, a shorthand that describes almost any idea that doesn't make sense or won't work, "That dog don't hunt." Making reference to pointers and retrievers, it's an apt way to think about start-ups that can't see opportunity in front of them. Remembering that every startup is really created to search for scale opportunity, you should operate with sufficient flexibility so that you are open to considering other ideas as you work on your original concept.

It is almost impossible to find a company that succeeded by making and marketing an unchanged version of its entrepreneur's original idea. New companies, like their new products, do not spring from the head of Zeus, perfectly formed. What a quarter of the world's population knows to be Facebook was not Mark Zuckerberg's initial vision of his company. "theFacebook," as it was known in its earliest life, started as a restricted Internet community to help students at Harvard and a few other colleges meet and date. Zuckerberg's pursuit of growth led him to see the ability of his platform to let anyone self-define a community within which they could share events in their lives. In short order, he realized that his company was reshaping the whole idea of communicating, and began to add feature after feature to make the platform an experience that would meet those needs. Once Facebook was supporting hundreds of millions of users worldwide, he redesigned the company as an advertising platform that is able to target individuals based on the topics that they follow.

Many of today's best-known tech companies began with completely different futures in mind. YouTube started as a website for people looking for dates; they could post videos and relate a little about themselves. When that formula wasn't working, its founders,

Chad Hurley, Steve Chen, and Jawed Karim, decided that a wider audience might share videos of anything and everything. Flickr began as a massively multiplayer online game, one feature of which, *Game Neverending*, permitted players to share pictures. Its popularity led to photo-sharing outside the game. Groupon, which provides great deals if a sufficient number of bidders materializes, started as a way to get users to support social causes. If enough donors expressed interest, The Point, its previous name, would gather donations to fund it.

Working with a too tightly focused view of your product may prohibit you from seeing larger opportunities. Meals to Heal started with one idea, but the entrepreneur, learning from her evolving experiences, including being frustrated by a market that just couldn't grow, discovered that her new company could pursue more promising products.

Recall Michael Levin's inability to morph his company to exploit the real opportunity that he had spotted—because his investors insisted that he follow the original plan that was not producing any revenue. When a survival opportunity emerged—a "mitigation opportunity" in the parlance of insurance—of shifting from steel trading to selling supply chain software, his investors resisted the chance to pivot to a new future.

Changing focus early to exploit a better idea often is the best way to mitigate the risk of failing. This is yet another reason not to have investors involved with your company until you have found a scale opportunity to exploit. If you have no choice but to bring on investors, minimizing their control can be very difficult.

## Avoid Stampedes

Many startups fail because too many would-be entrepreneurs suddenly seize upon the same product or service. Without a truly original idea, they are drawn to what seem explosive new opportunities, hot markets triggered by shifting trends in technology, the appearance of new business models, or the changing focus of investors and politicians. A decade ago, for example, discoveries relating to lithium-ion electrodes caused a stampede of startups making batteries. Similarly, thousands of companies were created to exploit drone technology. In the hypercompetitive markets that ensued, many failed.

A new business model also can set off a rush of emulators. In 2009, when Angry Birds showed that games for phone apps could be hugely profitable, a new industry grew up overnight. It is estimated that now more than three hundred thousand new game apps appear every year. Waves of startups in the same market space are common. All of a sudden companies selling bedding, pillows, monthly deliveries of cosmetics, bacon and beer, or discounted hotel rooms seem to appear all competing for what seems to be new customer demand.

Many aspiring entrepreneurs look to signals that they believe indicate shifts in investor interest. If it appears that investors are supporting startups in a new market segment, many aspiring entrepreneurs hurry to enter the space. A few years ago, a revolution in primary healthcare appeared to be underway. Venture investors, some of whom were not knowledgeable the healthcare sector, began to favor healthcare startups. One, Theranos, which had invented on-the-spot blood-testing equipment that could be employed in walk-in clinics, including in drug stores, gathered more than $700 million in backing. The concept was revolutionary, particularly in a medical world where blood testing is clunky and expensive, so its appeal was understandable. The problem was that, amidst the love affair with the idea, the testing equipment didn't produce accurate results. Even as Theranos melted down, investors continue to search for unicorns in healthcare.[4]

Changing government policy often generates entrepreneurial interest in new markets. The healthcare market seemed like a great place for startups when Obamacare became law. With its focus on novel ways of insuring people, its commitment to prevention, and the mandate to collect and employ patient data in pursuit of better health outcomes, many startups were formed. In the uncertain future of the Affordable Care Act, the future for these companies is quite suddenly clouded. Without significant government subsidies, the search for new patient care methodologies is uncertain.

Similar dramas have played out in the past. Federal initiatives aimed at reducing carbon consumptions were accompanied by federal grants and loans intended to induce entrepreneurs to start new companies in the space. Hundreds of companies were formed to advance state-of-the-art alternative energy production and use. Many appeared to flourish as long as government was stimulating demand by subsidizing power companies to buy wind turbines and solar panels. When government support ended, companies like battery maker A123, Abound Solar, which made thin-film solar panels, and Beacon Power, which built energy storing flywheels, failed. Of course, the catastrophic collapse of Solyndra, a company mass producing cylindrical solar panels, became a poster child for the subsidy problem.

There is little in the way of mitigating the risks that a startup faces in the midst of a stampede in pursuit of the same goal. Whether entrepreneurs are enraptured by a new technology, a novel business model, changing investor interests, or government incentives, chasing market trends, even ones initiated with billions of federal dollars, can be a dangerous pursuit. The rush of talent and money makes competing more difficult. Peter Thiel, a founder of PayPal and the first major investor in Facebook, warns that,

"Any fast-emerging industry can become so noisy that an innovation with real promise can't break through."

## Protect Your Idea by Growing It

Investors often want startups to describe the "barriers to entry" that a new company can claim. They want to know how difficult it will be for others to copy your great idea either while in development or, even more important, once it hits the market. What mechanisms or barriers will make it expensive, time-consuming, or otherwise too difficult for copycats to swoop in and grab the fruits of your labor?

Historically, patents have been viewed as the best protection. Once your startup's intellectual property has been recognized by the government, no one else is entitled to use it without paying you for its use, and you're in the position to refuse to sell and thus maintain your exclusive rights.

The presumed strength of patent protection in the United States has been gradually eroding in the face of multiple challenges, including from foreign competitors whose home jurisdictions may not recognize U.S. patent validity. For a startup, protecting and defending against patent infringement can involve expensive litigation that can drag on for years, a kiss of death for a lean startup and a system that now operates in favor of large companies that can afford teams of expensive lawyers. Is there a better way to mitigate the risk of having your idea stolen?

Increasingly the answer lies in developing your idea very carefully, testing markets as quietly as possible, and working through your startup's production and distribution mechanisms in anticipation of an all-in start, one that makes clear your intent to own the market that your innovation is targeting. Hamdi Ulukaya, the founder of Greek-style yogurt company Chobani, used this strategy to protect his idea. A Turkish immigrant whose family had settled in rural upstate New York, his first business was making feta cheese, a product that he concluded had a limited market and would not support his hopes of building a big company.

After studying the growing interest in healthy, lower-fat foods, Ulukaya decided to focus on yogurt. While yogurt had been introduced to the American diet in the 1960s and had been widely accepted in the market, there was, in Ulukaya's view, an opening for a better product—one that was lower in fat and offered the distinctive hook of being significantly higher in protein, in addition to providing a more substantial texture. In 2005, he bought a huge dairy plant in South Edmeston, New York, that had been abandoned by Kraft. For five hundred forty days and nights, he and a small team worked on perfecting the recipe for his product and retooling the factory to make nothing but Chobani Greek yogurt.

The new yogurt entered the market in 2007. Six years later, it was the largest producer of Greek yogurt in the country. Patent protection would not have been possible for Ulukaya, and he knew it; his recipe for yogurt, while unique, could be copied. Instead, Ulukaya decided he had to move fast and at a scale to become a major player so that other dairy producers would be caught off guard. That way, he could fend off competitors until he was firmly established in the market as the leading Greek yogurt.

## Hire a Great Manager

I hope that someday Professor Bruce German will be known as the scientist who improved the lives of tens of millions of newborns. A nutrition researcher at the University of California, Davis, German had studied mother's milk for nearly two decades. His breakthrough came in 2012, when he was comparing the microbiology of milk collected from around the world. German discovered that mothers in the developed world, who had routinely taken antibiotics prescribed for infections and colds since they were children, were producing milk that was deficient in several microbes that protect infants from a variety of diseases and conditions, including asthma, food allergies, obesity, Type I diabetes, and atopic ailments. What had piqued German's curiosity was that many of these conditions, so common in America and much of the Western world, are not found in children in the developing world.

German and his colleagues devised an ingenious prebiotic, a few drops of which, delivered just once shortly after birth, can help colonize the missing protective microbes in any newborn's stomach. Much like Franano, German's attempt to interest a major drug company fell on deaf ears. Companies reasoned that a one-dose drug would hardly pay back the significant development costs, including clinical trials.

After struggling for several years to successfully organize his startup, German concluded that he didn't know what was required to become a successful entrepreneur. More important, German realized that he was much happier working on basic research than working on a business plan; yet, he was passionate about getting a company going to make his formula and to undertake the arduous process of FDA approval. He decided to hire a professional CEO for the new firm, someone who had experience getting new compounds approved by the FDA. Within six months, German's new company had raised $10 million in venture funding and was undertaking the necessary research. Some day, Evolve Biosystem's prebiotic may be every baby's first meal. Consider the amount of human morbidity and mortality, and the enormous costs to society of the treatments for these life-long conditions. That situation may someday be diminished or eliminated because German was smart enough to know what he wasn't smart about.

# CHAPTER 9

# Don't Waste Time Doing Things That Don't Work

We all believe things that aren't true, deluding ourselves as to cause-and-effect relationships or harboring suspicions that just can't be. Championship athletes provide many examples. Michael Jordan wore a pair of lucky shorts, a carryover from his playing days at the University of North Carolina, under his Chicago Bulls uniform in every game of his NBA career. Before every home game, the famous Boston Red Sox third baseman Wade Boggs ate chicken, took exactly 150 ground balls during infield practice, and ran wind sprints at precisely 7:17 P.M. Turk Wendell, a relief pitcher for the Mets when they won the 2000 National League pennant, was known as "the most superstitious man in baseball." He chewed four pieces of licorice when pitching, brushed his teeth after every inning, and never stepped on a foul line. Female athletes are also susceptible to superstition: Tennis superstar Serena Williams always kept her lucky shower slippers close by on the court.

Athletes aren't alone in believing in fallacious causality. Richard Feynman, the brilliant and witty Nobel laureate in physics, gave the 1974 graduation speech at Caltech, which he titled, "Learning How Not to Fool Yourself." Feynman cautioned young scientists to steer clear of what he called "pseudoscience," which today we call "junk science." He pointed to all kinds of problems experts claim that they can solve, including how to reduce crime and cure mental illness, without offering any evidence that what they prescribe actually works.

These and many other theories that make broad claims have no effect on the phenomenon that they are trying to change. The needles just don't move. In fact, the gap between what we think we know and what we actually know is so big that we are susceptible to mistaking coincidence for causality.

In his speech, Feynman told a story about the people on a remote island in the Pacific who were as removed from twentieth-century technology as could be imagined. American forces operated an airbase on the island for a brief period during World War II. For a few months airplanes came and went, bringing supplies to the troops, who shared their food, beer, and other goods with the native population. When the war ended, the soldiers left, the airbase closed, and the supplies stopped coming.

Hoping the deities who had dropped the supplies would return, the tribe began to mimic the behavior of the departed troops. They maintained the airstrips and pretended to drive the abandoned jeeps. They made "headphones" out of coconuts, which they wore while sitting in the decaying control tower. They drilled in formation, wielding bamboo sticks as if they were rifles. In short, they invented what Feynman referred to as a "cargo cult." The islanders believed the soldiers' actions on the ground were the reason that cargo came from the sky.

Feynman's advice to his audience of young scientists was that, before they try to sell a proposed theory to others, they must eliminate all other possible explanations. He was warning the graduates not to promulgate findings that they could not substantiate by repeated tests: "When you have put a lot of ideas together to make an elaborate theory, you want to make sure, when explaining what it fits, that those things it fits are not just the things that gave you the idea for the theory."[1]

Feynman anticipated the problem with the implicit theory that currently guides many aspiring entrepreneurs. Many would-be entrepreneurs today wear a hoodie as a kind of talisman, in the hope that the gods of entrepreneurship will inspire them, as they did Mark Zuckerberg. They follow the steps they believe will result in a successful startup, including studying entrepreneurship in college.

## Engineering or Entrepreneurship?

As a high school senior, Denny Foster applied to college to study engineering, following in the footsteps of his father and brothers. He was smart, energetic, disciplined, a talented mechanic, and winner of his high school's robotics contest. If anyone was cut out to be an engineer, it was Foster.

After his second year, Foster decided to change majors and study entrepreneurship. He sought me out shortly before he began his junior year. Presuming that he was delivering me a compliment by emulating my career path, he proudly reported that he was leaving engineering behind and would spend the balance of his college career preparing to become an entrepreneur.

Before commenting, I asked if he had an idea begging to be turned into a company. He replied, not unexpectedly, that his new plan involved spending a fifth year on campus to work in the college's business incubator, where he would develop an idea around which to build a startup. He was surprised when I told him that he should continue in engineering.

Why did I give him that advice? For one thing, engineers start far more companies than graduates in any other major and, as a rule, they start a first business only well after leaving college. When I tried to discuss this reality, Foster dismissed my advice. He had already been seduced into an empirically false belief system, led on by professors and counselors who assured him that his college could instruct him in the surefire protocol of starting a successful company.

Foster can be forgiven for embracing this illusion. My simple advice, which I borrowed from Ewing Kauffman, is that the only way to learn how to start a company is to start a company. It sounds dangerously flimsy when compared to the detailed curriculum, exercises in how to write a business plan, and access to incubators that colleges now offer to serve the growing demand for training startup.

Nonetheless, like the hundreds of thousands of college students who study entrepreneurship, this student was a victim of academics who have made what philosophers call a "category mistake." They believe that teaching entrepreneurship, like teaching accounting and dentistry, involves imparting specific knowledge and skills that will dependably produce the desired outcome. They believe there is an empirically based core of knowledge that, once absorbed, will increase a student's chances of starting a successful enterprise.

These academics led Foster to believe that, if he took the prescribed courses and spent a year in an incubator, he would understand what entrepreneurs do. Foster had no idea that students who study entrepreneurship have no better odds of starting a successful business than anyone else. Nor did he know that the average lifetime earnings of students with a degree in entrepreneurship are the same as for most college graduates, but lower than those with degrees in engineering.[2] Foster also didn't know that businesses started by students immediately after graduating had a five-year survival rate of under five percent. If his academic advisers knew any of that, they weren't talking.

In short, Foster was unaware of facts that were highly relevant to his decision to change majors, primarily because most advocates for entrepreneurship studies suffer cognitive dissonance regarding these realities; it is a human tendency to shift factual interpretations to fit one's hopeful beliefs and preconceived notions. Unless the course is called "Owning and Operating a Successful Nail Salon in Atlanta," those who teach entrepreneurship cannot promise that they will give their students any special knowledge or any unique skills that will equip them to operate as professional entrepreneurs. They cannot provide that special knowledge because it is too circumstantial to be codified.

The nature of what entrepreneurs must know is different from what students who become accountants, chemists, and structural engineers learn in school. The essential "body of knowledge" imparted in these fields is based on observations that have been systematically tested, sometimes over centuries. Fact-based findings, tested repeatedly, have become rules that must be understood by anyone who aspires to practice these professions and to advance knowledge in these disciplines.

Accounting students gain knowledge by having to accurately calculate trial balances from real accounting data. Chemistry students must demonstrate that they know why the molecular weight of one atom explains why it will bond with another. Engineers must understand the strength of steel girders to a structure's ability to withstand an earthquake. The entrepreneur, however, cannot be taught in the same way as those studying a rule-based discipline. There is no time-tested body of knowledge that will improve the probability that a startup will be successful. There are a lot of practical common sense factors to weigh when deciding if the entrepreneurship path is for you, some of which are discussed in this book, but following rules or recipes does not work.

In contrast to those in the evidence-based disciplines, learning by doing is the only way entrepreneurs come to know what they know, much like surgeons or sculptors. Of course, those two fields require a thorough knowledge of anatomy or stone qualities, but the successful practice of surgery or sculpting depends on implicit or practical knowledge that resides only in the hands, acquired by experience.

Denny Foster naturally expected that anything taught at the college level would reflect empirically established causal relationships arising from years of scholarly research. But, in fact, what is taught in entrepreneurship classes largely is a system of belief in ritual practices that professors presume will lead to starting successful companies. The first thing that Foster was taught is that writing a business plan is the platform for all subsequent success—the *sine qua non* that will lead to a relationship with a venture capitalist, a godlike figure who will hold power over Foster's success. Foster was then instructed that working in an incubator would help him develop an idea around which he can form a startup. Finally, he learned that he needed a mentor, a Yoda-like adviser, to help him decode the secrets of starting a business.

In 1920, "Shoeless Joe" Jackson was tried for having taken a bribe to throw the 1919 World Series, which allowed the Cincinnati Reds to beat his team, the Chicago Black Sox. As Jackson left the courthouse, a devastated young boy, who, like millions of others, regarded Jackson as a hero, looked up at Joe, and begged, "Say it ain't so, Joe."[3] Unfortunately, college students who forego learning useful subjects and follow a course in entrepreneurship in the hope of learning how to start a company, might say the same. Can it be that what students of entrepreneurship are taught, the advice every aspiring entrepreneur hears, isn't all that helpful? What does the evidence show?

## Writing Winning Plans

A few years ago, when guest lecturing in a well-known MBA program, I spoke of the futility of writing business plans. A student in the front row began chuckling. When I asked him what he found amusing, he recalled taking an undergraduate entrepreneurship course where a written business plan had determined his grade. The professor, impressed with the young man's idea to build an online market for used dorm furniture, encouraged him to enter the school's annual business-plan contest, where potential investors, executives, and other academics judged the commercial potential of the contestants' ideas. The student had won first place, a cash prize of $25,000. His victory allowed him to compete against students from other schools in subsequent contests and, by the end of the semester, he had won three more, racking up $100,000 in cash, and a scholarship for the MBA he was pursuing.

The young man went on to tell his classmates that there was no way his idea could have worked and that while he was writing the plan, none of his fellow students would validate his idea. After competing in three contests, he observed that all of the processes shared certain unreal qualities. First, the judges seemed partial to socially responsible ideas, like recycling furniture, and seemed to subliminally signal that creating a company that would make money took a back seat to noble intentions. Second, most winning plans favored product ideas that served campus needs—a necessarily limited market—and the winning ideas thus seldom had potential to scale. Finally, he reported that judges tended to choose plans with detailed financial forecasts, no matter how unlikely the market uptake for the proposed products or services might be. He added that writing a winning business plan had been his first successful startup and was likely to be his last as he planned to pursue a career consulting for large corporations after completing his MBA.

In every business plan competition, prize money is awarded on the assumption that those who win have demonstrated top tier business ideas and will turn those ideas into startups. Experience shows, however, how unconnected most business plans are to actually building a successful business.

Consider that Rice University's business plan competition—the Super Bowl of such contests—awards in some years as much as $3 million of prize money, mostly in the form of offers of capital from wealthy investors. More than a thousand entrepreneurs apply to compete, but only forty-four are invited to Houston for the finals. Tellingly, only about thirty-five percent of all winners of the Rice competition have ever started a company. What little follow-up data exists on other university competitions suggests that an even lower percentage of those contestants turn their plans into startups.

Advising every aspiring entrepreneur to write a business plan appears to have very little predictive value as to who actually will follow through to start a business. These findings also support what we learned in Chapter 1: While case studies of individual businesses might suggest that a written business plan was useful in a particular instance or at a particular stage of development, there is no objective evidence that writing a plan has helped a large number of aspiring entrepreneurs.

That the debate over the value of the business plan is not yet settled tells much about how some professors of entrepreneurship think, which is too close for comfort to Feynman's cargo-cult metaphor. Few colleges keep track of their alums who study entrepreneurship, thus overlooking the single best source for evaluating the effectiveness of what is being taught. Moreover, university business plan contests, where the assumption is that the winners are those most likely to start successful companies, seldom track their winners' experiences, let alone compare it with that of students who lost, much less students who didn't even enter.

This lack of curiosity is intriguing. It suggests that business programs are convinced that what they teach is true, and that it need not be confirmed by examining their students' outcomes. In most university catalogs, writing a business plan is described as the capstone of what entrepreneurship students learn. And, whereas students in other disciplines are tested on their mastery of a body of knowledge and how that is applied in specific situations, grades in entrepreneurship courses depend on a professor's subjective assessment of the viability of the idea proposed in a student's plan—how well it conforms to the eleven-step convention and how convincingly the student can pitch his or her plan. Teaching entrepreneurship is a classic case of form triumphing over substance. As one student dryly observed, "If it ends with a grade, it won't end with a business."

## Recreating the Garage—Not!

Professors encourage students of entrepreneurship to spend time in a business incubator, where they presumably can discover or develop ideas for new businesses. Run as an adjunct—or, in Denny Foster's case, as an add-on—to formal training, incubators typically are nonprofit co-working spaces funded by local universities, businesses, chambers of commerce, and/or grants from government-funded economic development agencies. Often located in a commercial landlord's hard-to-rent real estate, the average incubator hosts twenty-five entrepreneurs who stay roughly one year.

Believing that aspiring entrepreneurs will cross-fertilize their ideas or form businesses together, incubators encourage social interaction among their tenants. Starting a business thus becomes a communal act. Every incubator has staff that host events and presentations intended to increase their tenants' chances of success. One common event is a "pitch night," at which entrepreneurs present their ideas to each other and to potential investors. Others include lectures by startup founders, hackathons to develop ideas for new companies, and workshops on topics ranging from how to file for a patent to sourcing goods from China. Incubators also offer access to lawyers and accountants who are ready to help cash-starved startups, in the hope that some will become future clients.

To visit an incubator is to have a sense of attending a perpetual social event, where the networking, connecting, and chatting never stop. Incubators make interactive theater out of starting a business.

The idea that incubators could increase the number of new startups was sparked in the 1990s, when Michael Porter argued that urban decay could be retarded in any city if it assembled a cluster of companies in a specific industry. He anticipated the larger idea of localized entrepreneurial ecosystems that emerged from AnnaLee Saxenian's 1994 book, *Regional Advantage: Culture and Competition in Silicon Valley and Route 128*,[4] in which she argued that the explosive growth of Palo Alto and Boston in the 1980s was due more to entrepreneurial activity than to the concentration of the computer industry.

Saxenian's book led hundreds of cities worldwide to replicate the institutional resources that they read as her prescription for growth. To benefit from entrepreneurial activity, a community needed a nearby university to provide a stream of innovation, as well as venture capital investors, but that was not enough. It also needed a place where aspiring entrepreneurs could work on transforming their ideas into companies, a scaled-up modernization of the garages in which companies like Amazon, Apple, Disney, Google, and Hewlett-Packard so famously got their start.

Much like the idea of business-plan writing, the theory of incubators would seem to make sense. Recall, however, that places dedicated to fermenting new businesses were not part of the startup landscape until relatively recently: In 1980, there were fewer than a dozen incubators in the United States; by 2016, there were more than 1,600.

Similar to other formal efforts to support entrepreneurs, it appears that, as a rule, time spent in an incubator is time wasted. As the number of incubators has exploded, the number of new companies being started has declined. The National Business Incubation Association offers no convincing data concerning its members' effectiveness in increasing the number of new startups or the number of new jobs they create. It appears that a significant majority of members do not respond to surveys about their outcomes.[5] In fact, the only published matched-sample study of the impact of incubators, compiled by Professor Alejandro Amezcua of Syracuse, relied on eighteen years of data, and concluded that "incubated companies have slightly lower survival rates than their unincubated counterparts."[6]

An aspiring entrepreneur who spends a year in an incubator is no more likely to start a company than those entrepreneurs who skip the incubator and go directly about the business of organizing a new company. Because the culture of incubators is designed to be encouraging, supportive, and mostly uncritical, an aspiring entrepreneur can spend weeks and months working on ideas that previously have been tried and failed or that have little prospect for market appeal. In that environment, it seems less, not more, likely that an aspirant will confront the reality of business startups and redirect his energy to potentially more productive work.[7] As a result, incubators—perhaps the most tangible and expensive component of the entrepreneurial ecosystem—appear to have a negative rate of return on the time that their tenants spend there.

Most aspiring entrepreneurs leave an incubator without a new business, usually because they had no consequential innovative idea when they arrived. They have spent months playing at business, much as children play house, and gone through the motions of being entrepreneurs, including pitching their business ideas to putative investors of ideas that are unlikely to grow into businesses.

This finding is consistent with studies of the effectiveness of the "big brothers" of incubators, entrepreneurial accelerators. Although similar in appearance to community-based incubators, accelerators are privately owned for-profit firms that initially were developed by venture firms to selectively admit aspiring entrepreneurs.[8] The accelerator often pays the aspiring entrepreneur's living expenses and provides resources to further develop their startups. Upon admission, entrepreneurs cede a portion of his startups' potential value to the accelerator's owners, who then choose which they will fund based on which embryo startups they believe will have the best growth potential.

But statistical evidence on accelerators, gathered by Seed-DB, suggests that they are no more productive than incubators. Using data submitted by seventy of the 160 accelerators that participated in its survey, Seed-DB concluded that only two percent of companies graduating from what it deemed the top twenty accelerators—a group that includes Y-Combinator and TechStars, the two most widely emulated models in the country—had "meaningful" exits where they were acquired or sold shares to the public. Moreover,

Seed DB concluded that it often takes ten years for an accelerated company to achieve success, just like most other startups.[9]

Y-Combinator, the granddaddy of all accelerators that started in 2005, accepts fewer than five percent of all applicants. Although less than ten percent of its hundreds of handpicked, highly coached, and financially supported startups achieve significant success, several notable companies have emerged from their system, including Reddit, Airbnb, and Dropbox. Nevertheless, the average rate of return on invested capital across all accelerators reporting their data, including Y-Combinator, is negative twenty-four percent. Despite the prevailing belief that accelerators can identify promising entrepreneurs and provide them with an experience that should result in a greater success rate, it appears that the accelerator model is no better at picking winners than are venture investors.

## Beware the Toxic Mentor

Aspiring entrepreneurs often hear that having a mentor, an experienced and reliable adviser, is critical to their success. The idea is based on the Greek myth of Odysseus, King of Ithaca, who asked Mentor, a wise and trusted friend, to watch over his son, Telemachus, while he was off fighting the Trojan war.

Unfortunately, when it comes to starting a company, mentors can be as dangerous as they are helpful. The reason lies in the seldom told second part of Telemachus' story.[11] Mentor, despite his promises and best intentions, couldn't protect Odysseus' son. In fact, Mentor's counsel was so dangerous that the all-knowing goddess Athena took on his identity to prevent Telemachus from following the real Mentor's advice. The moral of the myth was that Telemachus must find his own way in life. More colloquially, knowledge not gained through personal experience is often of limited value. The take away for entrepreneurs is that relying on a mentor can be risky.

My skepticism about mentoring was prompted while studying career paths in large organizations. I've seen versions of the following story play out several times. A CEO I knew well spoke often of the talent and promise of a young subordinate, whom he referred to as his "mentee." Eventually the CEO promoted the young man to vice president, setting him up to be his successor. Not long after the protégé was elevated to VP, he was unexpectedly recruited to be CEO of another company. Within a year, his new firm's board fired him. The mentor blamed himself for having made the path to the top too easy for the protégé; because of his favored status, he had never learned the necessary skills, including how to detect shifting political coalitions on his company's board.

Of course, a mentor's advice can be enormously valuable. A mentor might introduce you to a first customer, advise about an employment agreement, or suggest how to deal with an investor. Although some entrepreneurs believe a mentor shaped their success, such cases are the exception.

Franck Nouyrigat, a co-founder of Startup Weekend, is an acute observer of the mentoring process, and believes that mentors can be dangerous for entrepreneurs.[12] Nouyrigat argues that the mentor relationship in a startup setting always involves an asymmetric alignment of experience and interests, which can create four particular risks.

The first is that the presence of a mentor encourages delegated decision making. Because of the mentor's presumed wisdom, the entrepreneur tends to treat his mentor's advice as more trustworthy than his own judgment, believing it is drawn from years of experience that now should be applied to his startup. The urge to turn to others when making decisions in high-risk situations is normal. We do it with doctors and lawyers, for example, but they, of course, apply rule-based knowledge to reach fact-based decisions. This is not the case for startup mentors.

Mentors often step in, even when they are less equipped than their advisee, who likely has a better grasp of the dimensions, implications, and nuances surrounding the choices to be made for his new business. Psychologists know that once someone takes on an authority role, he feels obliged to answer questions to preserve his self-worth, even if he has no relevant experience. In short, the mentor may appear wise about things he knows little or nothing about.

Second, many mentors' advice is simply wrong. Like Mentor's promise to Odysseus, the counsel may be provided with the best interests of the entrepreneur in mind, but it reflects an inherent lack of knowledge. Every mentor draws on experiences accumulated at a different time and often in a different industry, or in the same industry in which the fundamentals have changed significantly. The founders of, say, Ask Jeeves, now Ask.com, a forerunner of Google, could give only limited advice to someone starting a search engine today.

Third, Nouyrigat says that some who assume the mentor role have ulterior economic motives that are not in the entrepreneur's best interests, resulting in what he refers to as a "toxic relationship." Many mentors attempt to leverage what they regard as their self-evidently valuable time and advice for an ownership interest in their mentee's company. The asymmetry of experience, age, and personal wealth gives the mentor an unfair advantage when making such a demand, as the entrepreneur might feel that the mentor should be rewarded for his volunteered time and input.

Once economically invested, however, the mentor may seek to maximize the startup's potential by assuming the role of co-manager. Sharing ownership essentially invites a contest over how to manage the startup, which can put the entrepreneur's vision in jeopardy. Some entrepreneurs have faced a draconian situation in which a mentor usurps the company.

Nouyrigat's fourth risk also is linked to satisfying the mentor's psychological needs. Many mentors see advising a young entrepreneur as a way to make their own lives more interesting, perhaps even more meaningful, but this is the last responsibility an entrepreneur should shoulder. This mindset is particularly troublesome among mentors who conflate their own corporate experiences with that of starting a company, perhaps believing that, when they were active in their businesses, they were "entrepreneurial managers" and thus understand how entrepreneurs think.

Confusing the situation yet more, mentors often are celebrated as altruistic, as giving back to the community. In fact, many mentors see advising a startup as an exciting way to spend their leisure time, one that can provide vicarious participation in the struggles of a startup, but without the risk they never took.

## Great Mentors Are Hard to Find

In the final analysis, Nouyrigat believes that mentors who can add genuine value to a new enterprise are very hard to find. Generally, valuable mentors don't see themselves as professional mentors or as members of a network centered around a local incubator. In fact, Nouyrigat suggests, the best mentors generally are reluctant to serve. Ewing Kauffman, who was an adviser to dozens of entrepreneurs, fit this model. He was happy to offer advice if asked.

Kauffman, however, knew that the burden of making a company work rested solely on the entrepreneur. He believed the entrepreneur's risk was personal and immediate and that those burdens could not and should not be shared by the mentor. Thus, he had a particularly useful view of how entrepreneurs ought to manage mentors: They should always operate on the premise that the nascent enterprise was their vision, that they held the information advantage, and that they were compiling information daily that would determine their company's trajectory.

In keeping with his view that your new company is *your* new company, Kauffman believed that an entrepreneur looking for advice should have more than one mentor, as hearing competing ways of thinking can widen the entrepreneur's perspective. In his view, having more than one adviser allowed an entrepreneur to regularly test the value of the advice offered and confirm that his adviser's knowledge and judgment remained relevant as the company evolved. Kauffman also believed that entrepreneurs should change mentors, and use different sources of advice at different points in the company's development. Kauffman often "fired" himself when he felt he could no longer make a useful contribution, which forced the entrepreneurs who sought his advice to make their own decisions. Finally, Kauffman never took a share of ownership in a startup if he was advising the founder, as he believed he could not render neutral advice if he had an economic interest. When I interviewed his former mentees, they were certain that one reason Kauffman's advice was so useful to them was that it was financially disinterested.

## Without Knowledge, Myth Reigns

As we have seen, the mechanisms that have evolved to support entrepreneurs have proven to be largely ineffective in producing new companies. In 1980, when the U.S. started more businesses per capita than we do today, no aspiring entrepreneurs wrote business plans or studied the process in college or practiced pitching startups to venture funders. There were no incubators and few venture-capital firms, and the idea of a mentor as a partner had not yet been conceived. Our nation's well-meaning but ill-conceived and expensive attempt to hothouse entrepreneurs has failed.

How this happened is explained by Malcolm Gladwell, who argues that there are instances when an idea or practice suddenly takes over our thinking. "The tipping point is that magic moment when an idea, trend, or social behavior crosses a threshold, tips, and spreads like wildfire."[13] The idea of formal efforts to induce more entrepreneurial activity was one such moment. As we saw, entrepreneurial ecosystems have become ubiquitous. Sometimes, however, the new idea that emerges on the other side of a tipping point is not always better. The cargo-cult-like belief in writing business plans, incubators, and mentors has made one of humankind's most spontaneous and creative acts, starting a business, into something resembling an industrial process: The right ingredients, if assembled correctly, should result in a successful startup every time.

This formulaic approach to starting companies rests on the fallacy that the imagined histories of a few highly successful technology businesses in Silicon Valley represent an optimal and universally reproducible model that any aspiring entrepreneur should follow to achieve similar results. But there is a problem inherent in building models this way. If we don't know which behaviors lead to which outcomes, entrepreneurs can end up looking as absurd as a tribesman trying to receive a radio signal through headphones made of coconuts.

Most of what is taught to entrepreneurs just doesn't hold water. The late Thomas Kuhn, a historian of science, might have said that a paradigm shift is beginning: We are starting to think about how new businesses really form.[14] Aspiring entrepreneurs need to be guided by advice that reflects how businesses start out in the real world. We have to abandon the current model of relying on plans and ecosystems because it doesn't work.

The excitement that greeted Eric Ries' book *The Lean Startup*, in which he advises aspiring entrepreneurs to skip writing a business plan, spending time in an incubator, and focusing on getting venture investors, suggests that others must be aware that the prevailing narrative is falling apart. Ries' simple prescription is to get a "minimally viable" product in front of customers as soon as possible and let them co-develop it with you.[15]

This is great advice for the software firms that Ries describes, but such firms count for perhaps two percent of all startups. For franchisees and merchant-entrepreneurs starting new stores— together more than eighty percent of all new companies—there is no such thing as starting lean. A building must be built, inventory purchased, and employees hired; thus, most startups are more properly characterized as "fat." Elon Musk's Tesla required billions of dollars of investment in engineering, a huge factory, and the parallel development of new battery technology before his first car took to the streets. Had he misjudged market acceptance, he would have choreographed one of the biggest business failures in history.

The next chapter proposes a better way for would-be entrepreneurs to go about starting a business.

# CHAPTER 10

# Planning for Success

How can you start a successful company? As we've now seen time and again, the secret lies not in writing formal plans. Planning, however, is a critical skill for every successful entrepreneur.

Everyone plans. Anticipating tomorrow's picnic, we buy beer, hot dogs, and charcoal today. Knowing that we have to pay college tuition for our kids, we start to save years ahead of time. An entrepreneur turns to planning in much the same way, anticipating needs and trying to have the resources necessary to shape the future of his startup.

As every entrepreneur discovers, however, planning a new business is more complex than most future events that we attempt to coordinate. In a startup, unless it's a franchise, very few of the factors that contribute to its ultimate success can be known up front. Every startup begins with an idea, a new product or service that must be developed and brought to the market. The new company can be thought of as a platform from which the entrepreneur searches for a scalable business opportunity, redesigning his product and constantly adjusting his resources to maximize opportunity and growth.

In this regard, an entrepreneur's planning is fundamentally different from how managers in large companies follow well-researched and formalized business strategies. Every big company has a history that defines what it makes, the industry in which it competes, its relationship with customers, and its historic growth rates. In big companies, planning is strategy. It is the formalized process, well understood by all involved, of how companies determine which paths to choose to achieve corporate goals. Thus, if the question is whether to build a more efficient factory, to invest in more innovation relating to a specific product, to jettison a line of business, or to acquire a competitor, such alternatives can be quantified and evaluated, one against the other, using financial and risk measures.

For startups, this type of strategic planning is useless. A startup exists to search for its niche in the market; then, its founder's initial idea, once tested and revised, will determine if the new company will even have a history.

The planning process in a startup can be described more accurately as situational decision making, an imperfectly informed, just-in-time, default strategy. The rapid and likely erratic evolution of events in a startup is so unpredictable that any other type of planning just won't work. Entrepreneurs must make decisions—often ones that prove, in retrospect, to have been of enormous strategic importance—on the spur of the moment, with little or no information, let alone algorithmic analyses of likely outcomes of one decision versus another.

Before exploring planning in an entrepreneurial context, it is useful to recall why strategic planning itself seldom succeeds. As the research of Hirschman, Kahenman and Tversky, and Bruner demonstrates, Pareto's Principle, also known as the "80/20" rule, is perpetually at work. Unwanted outcomes characterize eighty percent of plans both in corporate settings where, for example, acquisition synergies never materialize, and in planned public projects, where bridges and housing projects routinely cost more and take more time than forecast.

Strategic decision-making in most large corporations generally is reactive. Every business faces an unpredictable and dynamic environment in which critical matters change daily, making most strategic plans of limited practical utility. Obviously, rigidly adhering to a set of planned objectives in the face of market conditions that are shifting all around you is folly.

As we have seen, only about twenty percent of new firms survive for ten years, whether or not they had formal written plans at the beginning. Investing too much time and faith in the planning process is likely to make no difference for startups. As Billy Mann told me, "Planning is for big companies; they can afford to spend money on things that don't pay off."

## What Role Does Luck Play?

If startup success can't be planned, might it just be luck? Many entrepreneurs know that a single event made all the difference for their startup. The day an insurance executive told me that he had been waiting for my product to be invented, I knew that my first company could lead to a lucrative market. If I hadn't been lucky enough to see this possibility, my company would not have survived.

Andrew Smith had a similar moment when his company's future seemed to have been made on one sales call. Trained as an engineer, he wanted to find a way to use technology to improve the environment. While pursuing his MBA, he had been thinking about how over-the-road trucks could use less fuel. Smith had an *aha* moment when a camping equipment company set up an inflatable tent on the Dartmouth campus. He wondered if an inflatable device affixed to the rear of a tractor-trailer might reduce drag, thus improving fuel efficiency for the army of trucks that deliver most of our consumer goods. A little research suggested that even the toughest inflatable would not withstand the wear and tear of trucking.

But Smith wasn't ready to drop the idea. He experimented with toy trucks and pieces of cardboard to fashion miniature wind foils for the back of a trailer that could be conveniently folded to the sides by the driver during the loading/unloading process. Next, he built plywood prototypes that he affixed to a junkyard trailer. When it looked as if his design would work, he patented his product, calling it the TrailerTail, and sought investors. After graduation, Smith turned down a secure job with a major consulting firm and started ATDynamics.

But Smith's company, which now makes folding aluminum panels for trailers that are used by more than 350 trucking companies, almost died along the way. Previous attempts by others at making what are called "air spoilers" for trailers had acquired a stubbornly negative reputation among truck drivers and fleet mechanics. They believed that any device added to the rear of a trailer unnecessarily delayed loading and unloading times, and their experience was that the devices were prone to break, causing expensive downtime. While Smith had designed around these problems—his products required only minutes to fold out of the way and were nearly indestructible—resistance lingered in an industry not known for its eager embrace of new technologies. The TrailerTail was selling poorly and ATDynamics was burning cash at a rate such that, within a few months, Smith would have to call it quits.

On a sales call to Mesilla Valley Trucking in New Mexico, instead of being turned down as usually happened after Smith completed his presentation, the company's owner ordered 3,500 TrailerTails. At that moment, Smith knew that his company would be successful. He went back to San Francisco the next day to rebuild his factory and get going.

For many entrepreneurs, there is one "lucky" moment in their history on which their company's success hinged. For Art Ciocca, it was a bumper crop of grapes that save the day; Fred Valerino's future turned on his "bet the ranch" deal with one hospital. Without Lechmere giving him a contract for vending machines in all its stores, Bob Carlucci might still be running a pool hall. Howard Head's skis became ubiquitous once Killy was the first to cross the Olympic finish line. And, Billy Mann's luck was Céline Dion making a smash hit of one of his songs.

Some economists who have studied startups believe that luck is the most important determinant of entrepreneurial success.[1] Seeing luck as a principal cause of success, however, makes no sense; such a conclusion makes entrepreneurs into no more than irrational risk takers who invest years of hard work, foregoing the rewards of other career choices, all the while knowing that their fate will be decided by serendipity. If that's true, starting a business would require no more skill than playing the slots in Las Vegas— someone will eventually win. Yet, contrary to a commonly held view, studies show that entrepreneurs are more risk-averse than the population at large.[2]

## Lucky Planning or Planning for Luck

While there is no disputing the apparent role of luck in the success of many startups, fate similarly seems to determine the outcome of other human events. In the case of entrepreneurs, Dane Stangler, the former research director of the Kauffman Foundation, drolly notes, "Luck can't happen if you never start a business."

Entrepreneurial planning involves learning how to make critical decisions quickly, mostly about matters never anticipated, likely while relying on incomplete information. For entrepreneurs, planning is a real-time event much more often than it is a process of deliberate steps to be taken in a formulaic sequence. Entrepreneurs intuitively know that they have to be ready to recognize an unanticipated opportunity and make their own good fortune.

Becoming an entrepreneur involves acquiring experiential knowledge that only comes with practice. Someone aspiring to write a symphony can study music theory and orchestral composition in a conservatory but, to become a composer, you must write music. Surgeons often say they became surgeons on the day that they were first on their own in an operating room with no supervising senior surgeon present. Likewise, you never became a competent driver until you internalize the needed skills when driving by yourself, without an instructor.

Ewing Kauffman's observation rings true once again. There is no way you can know if you really are an entrepreneur, or can become one, by comparing your imagined talents or the quality of your innovation against other entrepreneurs. Rather, you must start a company. Then, whether your startup is successful depends on your ability to learn by doing and to understand the dynamic situation in which you have placed yourself, where every decision counts. Your startup has to survive long enough so that you can find your way to scale growth, and then you must manage your company so it becomes profitable and allows you to flourish. All of this requires a period of intense self-education.

## You Will Become an Entrepreneur All by Yourself

It is impossible to find an entrepreneur who does not reflect on his years building a company as the most intense learning experience of his life. Like Kauffman, every successful business founder learns every day how to build and grow his business. The learning and planning processes are inseparable. While the entrepreneur is learning-by-doing, he is determining his startup's future. Every step that the new organization takes is informed by what you have learned.

An entrepreneur's journey is essentially one of self-education, the acquisition of specific knowledge needed to be successful. Psychologists call this "inherent" knowledge, sometimes "the knowledge in your hands and head," which is learned only by experience. Just as in learning how to write music, do surgery, or drive, you must internalize the lessons needed for success.

This learning-by-doing model is the most effective way that any of us learn anything. Apple, one of the most innovative companies in history, recently rebuilt its educational support model around this insight. Many years ago, Steve Jobs launched the Apple Classrooms of Tomorrow program to maximize the impact of computers on student performance in the sciences. The effort relied on access to personal computers for every student and, as it developed, Internet connectivity in every classroom. After nearly two decades of experience, Apple learned that it wasn't enough to make the classroom a computer-rich environment with instant access to relevant information. The expected breakthrough in the learning process just wasn't happening, and student scores in the STEM subjects weren't improving. What was the problem?

Apple found that the most significant impediment was the traditional classroom method in which all students are expected to learn the same thing at the same time, with the teacher controlling the pace. Apple examined over twenty years of classroom performance data and engaged panels of educators from all over the country to work on the problem. The effort resulted in a second generation of the Classrooms of Tomorrow, one based on a new pedagogy model called Challenge Based Learning (CBL).

CBL enables individual students to teach themselves by identifying an educational challenge, a topic that holds particular interest or that a student just wants to know more about. The CBL model's effectiveness derives from every student coming to see her learning in the context of solving an important question, often contributing to the store of knowledge about the topic she chooses to study. The CBL approach has been proven to be a significantly more effective education model. And, as we will see, it reflects the way that successful entrepreneurs actually learn and plan.

Mark Nichols, the "father of CBL" who oversaw Apple's analysis and the discussions with its cadre of distinguished educators, told me that all of us learn the most useful things that we know by putting ourselves in circumstances where we must quickly acquire knowledge in order to make decisions. He used the example of the parents of a child who is beset by a debilitating medical condition. Using the Internet, the parents can quickly learn as much, sometimes more, than their child's doctors about the causes of the disease and its possible treatment, often becoming comanagers of their child's care and even strong advocates for new treatments or drugs.

Applying the CBL method, students set personal learning objectives to confront big questions, problems that anyone in the role of a student—which certainly includes a startup founder—might want to solve. The goal might involve building a rocket or designing and starting a company that sells specially formulated snack bars for sailors that both provide nutrition and prevent seasickness. By using a trial-and-error approach, learning what's needed to master the next step, the student or entrepreneur keeps adding to what he needs to know. Eventually, he reaches a solution that works or fails, sending him down a different path. The rocket flies or he goes back to the drawing board to redesign it; the nutrition bar is reformulated until some combination actually works.

Nichols believes that CBL's learning-by-doing method describes the innovative process that is implicitly employed at Apple when conceiving of breakthrough products. Many Apple innovations begin by someone describing a seemingly impossible challenge, a "stretch goal," something that is beyond what state-of-the-art technology permits. Steve Jobs was famous for asking—insisting—that Apple's engineers and designers create products that had never been thought of before and were impossible to make. The iPad is a perfect example. Most technical experts thought it impossible to sufficiently miniaturize computer technology to support its capability. Having established the undoable as its goal, however, Apple engineers had to deliver. Those who were involved said it was an exhilarating period of intense learning.

Apple's creative teams learn how to solve challenges by identifying, gathering, and applying the resources needed to achieve the required next insight. Along the way, of course, innovators recognize subsidiary problems and challenges that may themselves become new product opportunities that were never anticipated. The collateral innovation process reflects what the biologist Stuart Kauffman has called seeing "the adjacent possible," something that Michael Levin found when he realized that the software tool he developed to automate his new steel-trading business was the product that the market actually wanted.[3]

At Apple, Nichols points to a new program, its iOS Developer Academy, where CBL is being used to help students in several countries create new cell phone businesses. These students—all without any previous knowledge or experience with programming but who want to invent money-making phone apps—use CBL techniques to teach themselves iOS, the coding language of iPhone apps. Research shows that these students acquired iOS proficiency at least twice as quickly as students who learned iOS in conventional classroom settings. Many of the self-learners have created cell-phone apps, including games, and educational tools including one that teaches deaf people how to play the piano, that now are sold through the App Store.[4] Others have created their own application design businesses. Two years after completing Apple's CBL program in Brazil, one entrepreneur now runs an app support business in the city of Porto Alegre that employs fourteen people.

After studying students who used CBL to learn programming and start new businesses, Nichols believes that most entrepreneurs implicitly use the CBL technique. "It's an intuitive process, not one bounded by formal plans that cannot possibly anticipate exogenous events or circumstances." Nichols says that planning and learning are inseparable and codependent. In business, an entrepreneur, like any motivated student, is constantly compiling what he's learned to inform his next move. Planning is not a set of steps that are prescribed in advance to achieve success, but a dynamic, just-in-time process of learning and adapting.

## Fast Learning, Planning, Acting

No one knew this better than the late John Boyd, a brilliant Air Force fighter pilot who flew in the Korean War. Early in that conflict Boyd became frustrated that the North Koreans were routinely beating the United States in aerial combat. Boyd concluded that the Russian-built MIGs used by North Korea were simply better planes. Given that nothing in the way of improved aircraft was coming through the American military pipeline anytime soon, Boyd, a squadron commander, decided the only way to win was to train American pilots to become better at fighting the Korean MIGs.[5] Perhaps, he reasoned, if pilots could make better decisions in the midst of combat, they could improve their chances of shooting down their adversary before being shot down themselves.

Boyd devised a learning-decision approach known as the "OODA Loop." This involved the pilot *observing* the entirety of the situation around him, each factor that might influence his decision-making in combat. In aerial engagements before radar guidance, for example, weather conditions played a much bigger role than they would today. Second, the pilot had to *orient* himself relative to his opponent. What information could he assemble on how that enemy pilot was making tactical decisions? After a few encounters, was it possible to predict his opponent's next move? Next, informed by what he had seen as the air battle wore on, he needed to *decide* on his strategy, what his next steps would be. And, finally, he had to *act* repeatedly—pursuing and firing, adjusting his tactics each time using lessons he had only just learned.

As air combat in that era involved two planes closing in on one another at over 1,000 miles per hour, shooting seldom was on target during the first attempts.[6] As their duels continued, the OODA method helped American pilots learn and process sufficient information about their opponents to predict behaviors that improved their chances of success with each encounter. Boyd's method gave us the idea of learning through feedback, adding observations into an accruing framework by which to improve subsequent decision making.

Boyd, who never started or ran a business, realized the need for dynamic learning to improve performance and results. His methods are consistent with Apple's Challenge Based Learning Method in which, once a student envisions his big idea, he has to research possible paths to a solution, testing to see which approach is most likely to work, then choosing one and seeing if he can convince others of its value.

Both the OODA Loop and Apple's CBL rely on continuous iteration. As an entrepreneur, what you've learned so far can inform your next decision, helping you to assess your options against your evolving view of your startup's destiny, circling back to repeat and expand decisions and actions that work, or abandoning those that don't so you can try another approach. Applied in the context of starting a business, the Boyd-CBL approach describes a four step planning model used to manage four required resources needed for entrepreneurial success.

## Vision-Platform-Product Testing-Scale

Every successful startup continuously iterates among four processes: vision, platform, product testing, and scale. These basics can be thought of as a circle where, once the goal of the new business is laid down and a company is formed, they serve as a platform for testing ideas in the market that will lead the company to discover opportunities for scale growth.

Every company starts with the articulation of a vision, usually a new product or service. The entrepreneur or innovator sees the need for the "new" as a means to perform an existing process better, faster, or cheaper. His startup exists to manufacture the new product or provide the new service. In the case of a franchise, the idea is to bring an already tested concept to a new locale where customer needs are not yet satisfied. Whether it's your idea or one you rent, your new business operates as an instrument for sharing the benefits of a new idea with customers whose lives it will improve in some way.

No one knows at the outset, however, exactly how her idea will be valued by customers. Thus, every startup becomes a platform on which to develop and test the utility of an evolving product. This is where the bit-by-bit process of transforming an idea into a useful product takes place—a period of testing potential customer reaction. As we saw in the cases of Howard Head and James Dyson, hundreds of prototypes led them to their successful skis and vacuum cleaners. At the beginning, their companies, like every startup, were really workshops where their ideas continued to develop depending on how potential customers reacted to the functionality, convenience, and looks of their emerging products.

After what might be months or years of exposing your product to potential customers to improve it, the next step is to seek scale growth for your company. It is only by achieving size that you can secure your company's future and become self-sustaining. How long will this take? As we have seen in the statistics cited throughout this book, and in the stories of the entrepreneurs recounted here, knowing whether your startup will survive and then flourish generally takes from seven to ten years.

## Managing Four Necessary Resources For Success

To make these four processes most productive, you will have to simultaneously manage four resources: innovation, the people you work with, capital, and your company's competence in communicating with its market. The relative importance of these resources, one to the other, will vary over time. Situational planning involves knowing how to value and manage resources at a given moment.

Many people believe that success depends on one breakthrough idea. In fact, a fully formed market-ready product idea seldom springs from an inventor's head. And, as we have seen, more likely than not, entrepreneurs are building on and combining the previous insights and work of others. This is one reason that an aspiring entrepreneur who doesn't as yet have a compelling idea should consider taking a job in an existing company that has a track record of innovation. He will be up close to the process of innovation and in a context where he is more likely to see the need for an improvement or innovation in an existing product or process.

Because innovation itself is a progressive process, it must be managed. If your startup is formed around your own idea, it is imperative that you appreciate that, however wonderful you believe it is, it is unproven until it is exposed to potential customers. Your idea is never fully developed, even when it makes it to the market. When you bought your iPhone 5, you thought it was the last word in innovation. Even before its release, however, Apple already had set a challenge for itself: how to improve on its own most recent product. And it did the same with the iPhone 6.

The second resource you must manage is people. As your company starts, human resources play a role second only to your innovation. Without employees, you cannot make your idea into a concrete reality, something you can describe to investors. In the first days, you will have no capital goods such as machines to make things, nor will you have inventory or sales people to recruit customers. A startup is you and the first people you hire to make your idea take form.

Your people will and should command more attention than any other resource. With no room for error, you have to select and manage your first hires with great care. A few universal guidelines can help your planning by doing in this regard. As previously mentioned, you will likely confront the temptation to hire family members and friends whom you know, versus hiring strangers who might be better suited to the needs of your startup, but who seem higher risk precisely because you don't know them. There is no easy answer, but keep in mind, as already suggested in chapter 2, employees who are relatives and friends almost always present special challenges, particularly if they believe, based on their relationship with you, that they can claim a birthright to a job, along with outsized influence and outsized returns.

In a startup, you do not have time or resources to remediate employees who are not contributing as you had hoped and expected they would. Every successful entrepreneur learns to fire people quickly if they do not meet expectations, fit the culture of your organization, or can't grow their value to the company fast enough. You simply do not have time or the spare energy to deal with personnel dramas.

You should be reluctant to share ownership in the company with employees until they have proven their value over a long period of time. I am an investor in a growing startup where a talented CFO came to the company via another small company that the startup had acquired. After a few months of watching his new employer growing at an annualized rate of about 400 percent, the CFO proposed that he be recognized as a cofounder and insisted on an award of ten percent of the company's stock, which would have made him the first employee-shareholder. My advice to the entrepreneur was to fire him. Generally speaking, CFOs are fungible. More important, however, the implicit statement being made in his demands to the growing startup's owners was that their future success would depend on his input on every major decision.

Loyalty is a paramount consideration in deciding to keep an employee. Startups are yeasty places that breed ambition. You must be watchful that a highly self-regarding employee doesn't attempt to run away with your idea, customers, co-workers, or investors. Any seasoned investor, myself included, has seen a variation of this scenario enough times to know that honest dealing does not always pertain in startups.

Capital is your critical third resource for success. As we have seen, your initial stake most likely came from your savings, or from friends and family members who believe in you. As a result, it is imperative that you carefully manage your operating capital. Decisions about how you spend your operating capital—dividing it among product design and development, manufacturing, advertising, and sales, and on overhead, including rent and administrative costs—will decide the ultimate success or failure of your company.

The entrepreneur faced with running out of money, having burned through his operating capital before revenues can make the company self-sustaining, may blame investors who lose faith. While books and articles describe the drama of the Valley of Death, they seldom observe that a startup's demise is usually caused by imprudent application of resources and, even more likely because the entrepreneur's initial idea is not attracting sufficient interest in the market. In most instances, startups die because the entrepreneur could not describe a successful product that had scale potential. His original idea was not good enough and he could not find another idea fast enough that appealed to a bigger market. While it is hardly a "law of entrepreneurship," a good rule of thumb is that great ideas always find sufficient capital to be realized.

The fourth resource is the communications that you have with the market. How you take a prototype to market varies by the nature of your business. Eric Ries made a name for himself proposing the notion of "lean startup" that hinged around his experience with a software product that let his users co-design. The founders of Sheex tried prototypes with friends who they thought would be honest. Amy Upchurch bought advertising on Amazon's site to test the market uptake of her formula to overcome morning sickness.

Being able to accurately read market signals—how your current and potential customers use and value your products—is a critical corporate competency. Understanding customer reaction is critical in determining how your product might be modified to achieve greater market uptake and how to set prices to sell the maximum number of units that consistently make the highest profit.

Market competence is not the same as advertising your business. Many entrepreneurs make the mistake of believing that, if they can get sufficient press attention for their product, the way is paved for success. While media coverage likely won't hurt, no amount of advertising will help a product the market does not value for its utility. Further, the ease of generating "buzz" on the Internet has led many would-be entrepreneurs to misread real market reaction to their products. Much of what appears on the Internet about new companies and their products is generated, most often without effect, to attract investors. Great ideas get capital; bad ideas may attract a first round of investors but, without tangible evidence that large numbers of customers are ready to pay for your product, investors will abandon ship.

## Planning by Monthly Diary

You know that entrepreneurial planning is, by nature, situational. As you strive to find your path to long-term success, it is important to periodically self-evaluate where you are headed. Review the condition of your startup monthly, being as dispassionate as possible in assessing whether you are on a path that will lead to scale growth. The discipline of a periodic review of your startup's status and potential, which really is "planning as you go along," should be part of your management practice. Build a brief analytic template, no more than four or five written pages, accompanied by several separate spreadsheets, that make an ongoing record of your progress and your plans for the upcoming period. This document is the diary of your startup.

Your summary of progress should describe in precise terms the state of your innovation and the actual status of your product at the reporting moment. Carefully record what is causing your product to evolve. Note how your research is progressing, including how you are responding to specific customer needs. Document how you have gathered systematic market feedback. Write down your record of various prototype trials and the outcomes they produced with what types of customers. What are the specific next steps that you believe will provide valuable information to you about what will make your product more successful?

Of course, you will want to list your customers, if you have any, and what sales or income you can expect from each. These estimates should be written down on a separate spreadsheet and checked every month against previous estimates to determine whether you are misleading yourself about the potential of your product. Whether you have customers or not, you should be developing specific views as to who will buy your products, at what price, and whether the revenues from those sales will sustain your company.

Next, you should record any formal market commentary on your product. Are there news stories, discussions of your product in trade magazines, newsletters, or online? If so, are they helping your sales efforts? Should you be dampening premature discussions of your products and the supposed progress of your company to protect your idea, or should you be encouraging it to build your brand?

Throughout all of this, you must track the financial status of your company, how much money you have, what your sales and expenses have been. What's your burn rate—how many months can you survive with the money on hand? Once again, you've got to go back to your previous forecasts to see if you are improving your performance. Do you need to be approaching investors, emphasizing more sales, or cutting expenses?

Finally, you should constantly evaluate your staff. Until you have reached a critical mass of about thirty employees, you should be judging the contribution of each individual to your company's progress and note what you expect of them in the next phase of the company's growth. (After thirty employees, this analysis likely needs to become more formalized.) Do your previous assessments of an individual suggest that he or she is becoming more or less valuable? Write down your intended personnel decision and, later, remind yourself why you did or did not execute against your plan.

Every year, you should review these monthly diaries to see if you are making progress against your vision, or figure out how you can plan for more luck.

# CHAPTER 11

# Becoming a Successful Entrepreneur

Professor Mike D'Eredita of Syracuse University has a unique perspective on how to train entrepreneurs. As a rowing coach with a worldwide reputation for helping struggling crew teams, D'Eredita always has some country's Olympic hopes in his hands. He also is an entrepreneur, having invented a rowing simulator. One of his machines is used by Frank Underwood in the Netflix drama *House of Cards*.

All athletes must learn the rules of the games that they play. Of much greater importance to competitive athletes, however, they must develop winning skills. To prepare Olympic athletes for competition, statisticians use big data to identify the best techniques to improve performance. Swimmers, rowers, sprinters, and hammer throwers keep setting records because the techniques of thousands of previous champions have been studied in great detail, resulting in improved dolphin kicks; the ideal timing, depth, and angle at which oars should enter the water; new insights about the best ways to push off the track's starting blocks;

and the perfect way to spin and release a sixteen-pound weight to achieve maximum distance.

Athletes with potential are identified the same way. Olympic coaches study the race results and game performances of tens of thousands of high-school and college players in a search for competitors with enough raw talent to compete at the highest level of a sport. A handful of prospects are invited to Olympic training camps. Those ready to commit to what can be several years of training in pursuit of Olympic glory are drilled in the latest techniques that will increase their likelihood of winning. Athletes and coaches are carefully matched; prolonged and intensive interaction requires personalities that fit well. Only athletes who constantly improve during training are invited to continue.

In our discussions of the fact that incubators and accelerators fail to increase the chances of entrepreneurs starting successful companies, Professor D'Eridita wisely observed that, "If we trained our Olympic Athletes like we train our entrepreneurs, America would never win even a bronze medal."

You know now that writing business plans won't lead to success. And, as D'Eredita's observation reminds us, there are no training-camp equivalents that can teach you how to be an entrepreneur or teach the best techniques or "moves" to increase your chances of success in starting and managing a flourishing new business.

Advocating to the contrary, however, are endless Internet lists of authoritative "dos and don'ts" for anyone hoping to start companies. Not surprisingly, many contradict each other. Erstwhile entrepreneurs, maybe successful and maybe not, journalists, professors, investors, and observers up in the stands, with no experience playing the game, offer opinions about what you should know and do to create a winning startup.

Absent an Olympic-style recruiting and training experience for would-be entrepreneurs, what can you do to increase your chances of success? What follows are my views of what successful entrepreneurs do to build great new companies that survive and flourish. These ideas are distilled from the stories in this book to the basics of what might be called the "science" of startups. They reflect my experiences founding companies as well as what I've learned meeting and talking to thousands of entrepreneurs before, during, and since my ten years at the Kauffman Foundation. In addition, these observations reflect what can be gleaned from the large databases that Kauffman funded to capture the history of thousands of startups. I have watched the game, played it myself, studied how others might increase their chances of winning, and helped others play by providing investment capital.

To illustrate these lessons, I chose the entrepreneurs in this book to stand in for the average Everyman entrepreneur. Each created products, and then the companies to make them, that have improved the lives and happiness of their customers, including many of us.

## 1. Be Ready When Your Entrepreneurial Moment Comes

Most of the people who you have met here can be described as "accidental" entrepreneurs. In fact, few set out to create their own businesses; their ideas to start companies were inspired by seeing innovations that had the potential to reach wide swaths of customers whose lives could be made safer, healthier, more convenient, and even happier by the speed, labor-saving, or pleasurable nature of their ideas.

Entrepreneurs most often are the creatures of circumstance. Art Ciocca was so disappointed with Coke's decision to sell off the division that he had rebuilt, which he saw as poised for a great future, that he found himself buying the company. Ciocca vividly recalled that his career goal had been to climb the corporate ladder to head a major food company. Fate, however, laid open a very different opportunity.

Patrick Ambron was not a wannapreneur, driven by a career dream of graduating from Syracuse University with a startup under his arm. Only by trying to help his roommate find a job did Patrick start down that road.

Of course, Art and Patrick, like the other entrepreneurs we've met, took up that challenge when others in their situations might have demurred. More likely than not, there is nothing special in the psychological make up of entrepreneurs that predicts who will embrace an opportunity that comes their way. Entrepreneurs are not business daredevils, they are not race-car drivers. Rather, they seem to have been in the right place and at the right moment in their careers when a good idea, which they decided was worth pursuit, came into view.

Nonentrepreneurs may be people unlucky enough to never have seen the need for an innovation. Or maybe they simply couldn't envision that they ever could start and run a company. Perhaps, at the moment in their lives that an entrepreneurial opportunity or inspiration presented itself, they were not free to take up the challenge of a startup or to pursue a promising innovation. But, if you think that you might be an incipient entrepreneur and are inclined to be on the lookout for your moment, you should work to predispose luck to break your way. That could include saving money to invest in your startup and to cover the loss of income when you step away from your day job.

## 2. Make Innovation Happen

In the rush of excitement that comes with launching, many startup founders make the same, ultimately fatal, mistake: They ignore the reality that every new company needs a good idea. Startup failure rates are rising, in some part, because too many people are starting companies with ideas that just aren't viable. It may look great on paper but will—sometimes very quickly—fail the market test.

As we've seen by now, innovation doesn't come in for a landing on schedule. Most aspiring entrepreneurs can't know when or where their great idea might arise. Many, particularly younger entrepreneurs, inspired by the "garage" myth, believe they can force a radical breakthrough if they mimic what they know about how other innovators came up with their ideas. They usually don't know that most startups are the makings of middle-aged entrepreneurs who bring technical knowledge, as well as lots of business and industrial experience, to their task. With no appreciation of this, young aspirants are more likely to believe that novel products with no perceivable value to buyers will somehow catch fire once they hit the market. They imagine that people will realize that they really do need an app-controlled frying pan, a folding sailboat, or some other hardly believable thing. These naive entrepreneurs play something like startup roulette.

The difference between those who succeed and those who fail seems, in large measure, to be an individual's inherent sense of how the innovation process works and how to implement that process. Good ideas take time to appear and be refined. They emerge slowly from what the innovator already knows, reflecting his ability to plug diverse pieces of technology or information together in new ways. Once a new idea has crystallized, it feeds the ongoing synthetic process. Innovation begets innovation. Again, this is why so many entrepreneurs are in their forties when their inspiration comes. Years of exposure to relevant technologies have shown them how innovations unfold from combinations of existing products and processes to make something new. And, once entrepreneurs like this have one good idea, they are more likely to have others.

"Everything comes to him who hustles while he waits." That spot-on advice is attributed to Thomas Edison.[1] If you are feeling the sense that you might be destined to start a company, look for opportunities right under your feet. "Hustle" in the circumstances in which you find yourself.

Pevco's Fred Valerino has filed an average of three new patents a year since he began redesigning pneumatic tubes. He didn't start his company envisioning that he would become an inventor; it happened more as a necessary response to emerging customer needs. Valerino learned how to speed up his inventive abilities. Like most successful companies, Pevco became an innovation platform for a constantly improving technology that keeps the company growing.

The model for this phenomenon may be Thomas Edison himself. It took Edison nearly a decade to perfect his light bulb, which generated only fourteen patents. When the light bulb was able to replace dangerous gas light in homes, Edison conceived of building a "grid" to bring electricity to buildings in lower Manhattan, his test market. The process required an intensive and nonstop period of innovation, solving problems as they emerged during the development of the first electric utility company. To make his dream a reality, Edison had to invent dynamos, transformers, regulators, switches, magnetos, meters, and fuses—the entire kit needed to light up one part of New York City. His grid served as his platform for innovation. Edison patented nearly four hundred inventions related to the generation and transmission of electricity, and his work provided a technological blueprint for the world's future. For decades, General Electric, Edison's startup, was regarded as the most innovative company on earth.

From the perspective of Albert Hirschman, the theorist who proposed the planning fallacy, the pace of innovation under pressure would not be surprising. In Hirschman's study of planning, what separated failure from success was the ability of project managers to behave like entrepreneurs, creating solutions as if out of thin air to stave off organizational failure. Hirschman's study suggested that, in most cases, the "hustling" approach required a manager to deviate substantially from the solution envisioned in the original plan. Entrepreneurs become innovators once a project is underway, mostly to stave off failure. Many times the plan itself holds the seeds of failure; recall how Michael Levin was locked in by his investor's plan. He couldn't pivot to capture an opportunity that arose from his original innovation.

Of course, the returns on hustling while you wait are also enjoyed by entrepreneurs who, in one sense, play it safer. They buy franchises, tried and tested business ideas that come with detailed business plans. As we saw in the case of Bob Carlucci, once up and running, his franchises proved to be the seed of much larger businesses, which then inspired more new ideas. While he adhered, as required, to the franchisor's required plans, he built adjacent businesses where he could invent new solutions to increase the efficiency of all his businesses, including a construction company and a bank.

## 3. Be Realistic About Time

Before Proteon failed its FDA Phase 3 clinical trials, Nick Franano told me that, if he had ever known that it would take sixteen years before he would know if his company would succeed, he would never have started it. Nick, like every entrepreneur, was bullishly optimistic about a timeline. Of the thirty percent of startups that survive past five years, most are not profitable until they reach their seventh anniversary. Successful companies that go public sell shares on average after they are more than eleven years old.

Yet, the average proposed time to cashing out, an "exit" in business plan parlance, is four years. Having read thousands of plans, I have never seen one propose that prospective investors would have to wait ten years to get their money back.

Every entrepreneur wants to start a "unicorn," one of the handful of companies whose great idea is so powerful that its life cycle is measured in months, and the selling of which in a few years provides a check denominated in billions. This is not likely to happen to you. In James Dyson's words, your experience starting a company is more likely to be a "long slog." The dream of success should sustain you, but understand how long and hard the path may be.

## 4. Build Your Company as Your Life

Remember how Susan Walvius, the co-founder of Sheex, described the differences between starting a company and coaching basketball? She said that basketball was easy by comparison: "You practiced, played, and either won or lost." In business, she observed, the game just keeps going with no ending buzzer. "There's no just getting through forty minutes."

Walvius told me this seven years after she and co-founder Michelle Brooke-Marciniak started their company. While they had no idea what the future might hold when they began, they knew that if they were giving up coaching, a profession they loved, they wanted to start a company that would be around for a long time. What lay ahead was just as tumultuous as they had expected it to be. They had to learn quickly how to contract for fabric production in China, and then how to move manufacturing from one company to another to maximize quality. For two people who had never been abroad except as tourists, they were suddenly faced with figuring out who could be trusted, how much things really cost to make, and how to move raw materials and finished goods from one country to another. Many crises tested them: suppliers broke contracts, shippers didn't deliver on time, and a major distributor went bankrupt. At times they weren't sure if sufficient product demand would ever exist to keep Sheex alive.

How did they keep going? There is something in the success of a new venture that correlates with the motivations of the entrepreneurs. From the outset, most successful entrepreneurs know they are creating businesses that will define their lives—and not just by how much money they might make. Without this intense personal connection to the idea behind the company, a startup founder will have a hard time summoning the persistence necessary to plow through the inevitable rough patches. And persistence, we know, is one of the hallmarks of successful entrepreneurs.

Throughout my years of meeting entrepreneurs, I always have been impressed by how many successful founders see their companies as living extensions of themselves. This is not surprising; many of us take our principal identity from our work. We know ourselves, and others know us, as bankers, sales reps, chefs, or mechanics. As an entrepreneur, your company will begin to define your identity, and your life will be all about building a company to make better helmets for bike riders or collapsible travel cages for dogs. Making your company survive and become successful will be part and parcel of your personal growth and will shape your character. This is why many entrepreneurs appear to have been born to the task. They are doing something that seems authentic to their lives.

Eighty percent of firms fail before getting to the magic ten-year mark when, on average, they become self-sustaining and begin to experience scale growth. Those that survive are seldom sold. Over ninety percent of twenty-year-old firms are still owned by their founders. Think about James Dyson and Fred Valerino and their now decades-long relationships with their companies. They are like Jeff Bezos and Mark Zuckerberg, who go to work every day in the companies they started. It can't be to make more money; Bezos and Zuckerberg are among the richest people on earth. Instead, they are testing and pushing their ideas to shape and discover the future of their companies—and their own destinies. Successful entrepreneurs often have a hard time envisioning a future in which the company they founded doesn't play a central and exhilarating role in their lives. Great entrepreneurs start companies to grow companies, not to sell companies.

## 5. Be All In

Certainly, starting a company is not for the faint of heart. Because of the high likelihood of failure, as many as seventy percent of all new entrepreneurs attempt to mitigate the risk of starting a new business by continuing to hold down a full-time job. Being a part-time entrepreneur, however, is highly correlated to a lower probability of success. The obvious reason is that becoming economically dependent on their startups makes entrepreneurs work harder to achieve success. So certain is he that an entrepreneur must be entirely committed to his startup that Paul Graham, the founder of Y-Combinator, once observed, "If startup failure were a disease, the federal Centers for Disease Control would be issuing bulletins warning entrepreneurs to avoid day jobs."

## 6. Learn To Manage Chaos

While all management is difficult, trying to steer a startup, which has no established product, no place in the market, and is perennially under-resourced, is particularly daunting. With little or no management experience, an entrepreneur suddenly must make decisions in one of the most chaotic situations ever.

When I asked Susan Walvius how she and Michelle Brooke-Marciniak had managed Sheex through the company's turbulent first years, when they had no clear signal from the market that the company could be successful, she drew parallels with the way coaches deal with tense moments of a game when the outcome could go either way. While every coach and every startup manager has to make decisions on the fly, there are tricks that can help you in managing through the chaos.

The first is to make brutally efficient use of your time, and figure out a way to get as much of it as you can. In the last minutes of a tied championship game, with thousands of fans yelling and all your players desperately looking to you for the right play, managing the clock is critical. Every coach caught up in a tight game knows that the best weapon can be a "time out," where she can change the flow of the game, disrupt the other team's momentum, and re-establish her own strategy.

Entrepreneurs have to believe that, with enough time, they can solve any problem. How to get more time? While time can't actually be slowed in real life, most successful entrepreneurs seem to figure out how to manipulate events and conditions so that they play out at a more manageable pace. Many entrepreneurs have told me they retreat to a quiet mental space where they can work through a problem away from the hubbub. Once there, they can reconstruct facts and decide which problems are so critical that they must take priority. They might reshuffle who they consider to be as their most important customers, which suppliers might agree to wait for payment, or, among their investors, who is the most likely to write the next check. In the midst of tumult, all decisions come down to figuring out what you must do right now and what can wait.

Second, be decisive. Managing mayhem requires the entrepreneur to abandon what might seem like normal causal logic, getting caught up in what seems to be the correct or ideal sequence of events. Crisis requires action. The if-then order that our brains tend to impose on decision-making has to be interrupted. Chaos is often best dealt with by getting to the "then"—the outcome of the action—rather than waiting for the ideal preconditions to present themselves. There are times in a basketball game, for example, that the right advice to players is not to wait for the other team to set up their expected defense, but just to play to the basket.

Finally, do more of the things that you know, from experience, will make a difference. They are the same three things in every business: Step up your interaction with the market, that is, your sales; strengthen the team you have working with you, your people; and, improve how the world regards your business, your reputation.

## 7. Help Your Customers Like Your Product

In my first company, I stumbled upon one of the greatest lessons any entrepreneur can learn—test the value of your product to potential customers as early as you can. I had invented a way to analyze any hospital's performance compared to similar institutions. Never having worked in a hospital, however, I was not sure how my target customers might want to "see" such information. I began to visit hospital administrators and asked them to help me design reports that they might use to convince doctors and nurses that other institutions were operating more efficiently, really caring for patients in better ways. I went through dozens of designs for reports with twelve hospitals before I took my product to market. In retrospect, it should have been no surprise that ten of my "trial" hospitals became customers—my product was their product.

Howard Head knew that his potential customers didn't know that they needed his new skis. He was perpetually frustrated that he couldn't produce enough skis fast enough to get people to see how much more fun they could have if their equipment was better. Even when he did, customers continued to prefer their traditional wooden skis. Why? "It was just the way things were supposed to be."

If cracking the skiing market was hard, tennis was yet more difficult. The sport had been the preserve of country-club players who embraced its traditions, including its equipment. Tennis was steeped in formal rules. Players, by convention, wore white shorts, white shirts, white socks, and white shoes, and played with wooden racquets with catgut strings.

Head knew that everyone would ski and play tennis better with his products, but he came to understand the world needed help to figure this out. He decided that old-fashioned product endorsements were still important and that the best way to accelerate demand was to identify his products with promising and attractive young players.

Another entrepreneur who discovered promotional endorsements is Kevin Plank, the founder of Under Armour. Like Head, Plank first sold his line of sports apparel to football players from the back of his car. Through a lucky circumstance, a friend convinced Jeff George, then the Oakland Raiders' quarterback, to try one of Plank's shirts. After George was pictured in *USA Today* wearing Under Armour, demand shot up. Plank learned that branding, showing his innovative product being used by others, was the key to winning customer loyalty.

Head once told me that he was always torn between "good enough" and perfection. Both he and James Dyson had made technical breakthroughs, but they wanted to deliver more than just better functionality to their customers. They wanted to make their products beautiful.

Steve Jobs was similarly committed to the pursuit of beauty in his products. He wanted every Apple customer to feel that they had acquired a piece of art—sleek, subtle, and suggestive of the power of the unlimited intelligence to which it helped to connect users. Jobs knew that, like computer makers, car manufacturers compete on technology, but that great design explained market share more than horsepower or fuel efficiency.

Jobs, like Head, Dyson, and Plank, understood that the more he knew about his customers, the better his business decisions would be. Anyone who has ever visited a Whole Foods Market has encountered a budding entrepreneur handing out free samples. More than ready to talk with you, he is testing market reaction to his new gluten-free cookies, or the fruit and nut bars that he formulated for runners, or his faux-chicken soup made with tofu. Every year, about eighteen thousand new products are introduced to grocery stores, but only eight hundred will make it into inventory. The entrepreneur wanting to chat you up, to provide you with something to eat, is attempting to see if his imagined "target demographic" includes the customers actually taking his new product home. If not, his dream may be going up in smoke right there in the cracker aisle.

## 8. Guard Your Reputation

Once your company is up and running, you must manage its reputation. How it becomes known comes down to whether or not you can deliver what you promise. Is your product all that you say it is? Do you deliver on time? Do you deal with defects quickly? Do your customers say great things about you? Do you have repeat purchasers?

You know the old saying: "You don't get a second chance to make a first impression." It's true. Once you have a reputation for selling a flawed product or for being unable to fulfill customer demand, it's almost impossible to dislodge a negative image from people's minds, much less from social media and other online sources. I once was an investor in a company that developed problems keeping up with product demand. Years later, wholesalers continued to think of the company as slow to fill orders, even though the supply problem had long since been remedied.

## 9. Practice Before You Start

Many entrepreneurs consider starting a company for years before they actually take the leap. While they may be moved to do so by a specific opportunity, it appears that, subliminally, they had been considering for years how to work for themselves or how owning a business could be their right next step. This contemplative pre-entrepreneurial phase doesn't get much attention; as I've noted, the popularized misconception is that business ideas come on like brainstorms and, once someone has one, they can't help but charge forward.

Perhaps this is why, until recently, there have been few resources to help nascent entrepreneurs get a feel for what starting a business might be like, or even how to meet and talk with entrepreneurs who have made the decision to start a company. Fortunately, a few newly created programs exist to help those who are considering starting a business, even if they don't yet have a fully formed concept. These programs help people become familiar with the world of entrepreneurship. They exist to help you recognize whether you are likely to take that plunge, what it might feel like, and what you should do about it.

The most widely available program, now operating in 110 cities, is the Kauffman Foundation's 1 Million Cups. An informal weekly gathering usually held on Wednesday mornings in a local cafe, the program is open to anyone interested in meeting with local entrepreneurs who, just like you, once wondered if they should start a company. This is the best program if you want just to get a feel for what entrepreneurs experience, what they think about, and how they plan to grow their new companies. Most sessions involve an aspiring entrepreneur pitching an idea. Unlike business-plan competitions, however, where the proposed innovation is relatively settled, at 1 Million Cups events most of the presentations are early descriptions of ideas to gather reactions and input from the general audience. No one is obligated to join; you can stop by once, become a regular, or even try out an idea yourself. To get a virtual feel for the process, examples of pitches are archived at the Kauffman Foundation's 1 Million Cups website,[2] and you also can find upcoming meetings.

The Startup Weekend program also provides aspiring entrepreneurs with a perspective on starting a company, but in a more intense simulation experience. Anyone can sign up for the fifty-four-hour experience; an average weekend involves about eighty strangers working together through three days of exercises. On Friday, participating individuals describe their backgrounds, outlining their industrial knowledge and skills, any new product ideas they have, and why they might want to start a business. On Saturday, individuals form teams that reflect shared backgrounds or similar interests in new products. Groups discuss and research ideas, build prototypes using common objects like LEGO blocks, and test their ideas with other participants. This purposefully fluid process encourages individuals to clarify and float ideas in a low-risk environment, creating and joining new teams throughout the weekend. On Sunday, all participants listen to five-minute pitches, which often set off new rounds of development.

Since 2007, nearly 200,000 individuals have attended these weekends. While their purpose is only to expose entrepreneurs to the process of starting a new business, more than two thousand startups have emerged from the experience.[3] One, Zaarly, a cross between Angie's List and Craigslist, provides a matching service for customers and vetted individuals for "gig" work. It raised more than $12 million in venture capital in its first three months.

Another community resource is the Blackstone LaunchPad program. The initiative was created during the 2008 recession to help University of Miami graduates who were having a hard time finding jobs. The idea was to teach them to create a company as a means of making their own job. Established as part of the school's outplacement program, it is nondirective and operates without a curriculum or formal programming. Rather, using a technique much like Apple's CBL, participants learn by quickly surveying ideas that might be developed into new businesses. They gather as much information as they can about an industry, its marketplace, and what makes companies in the space successful. In some ways, it is like an extended session of Startup Weekend.

Through these LaunchPad programs, university alumni play supportive roles in helping students with their startups, providing introductions, and, in some cases, becoming first customers. While generally located on campuses, the programs and their resources are commonly open to anyone in the greater community. In its first eight years, the University of Miami's program has birthed more than four hundred companies and created several thousand jobs. Initially funded by Kauffman, the Blackstone Foundation has sponsored new LaunchPad community sites on twenty-five campuses.[4]

Although operating in only a handful of cities, TechShop allows anyone needing prototyping facilities to use a completely fitted-out machine shop.[5] Among the many tools that innovators and entrepreneurs can find on site are 3D printers, laser cutters, wood- and metal-working machines, welding facilities, printing presses, looms, and sewing machines. Similar machine shops exist around the country, part of the emerging "maker movement," where entrepreneurs can build prototypes and, in some cases, make their products. The Toronto Public Library, for example, operates a community machine shop, harking back to Andrew Carnegie's vision that public libraries were a critical resource for stimulating more industrial innovation in their communities. Many universities are opening prototyping facilities as well. While generally limited to students, some allow access to community members working on entrepreneurial projects.

## 10. There Are No Rules and You Are Playing for Keeps

Many aspiring entrepreneurs approach the possibility of starting a business after seeing that an enthusiastic community support network is ready to assist them. In fact, as many as 100,000 people work in programs operating at the local level that are aimed at encouraging entrepreneurship. Despite the fact that there is no evidence of their effectiveness, community incubators and business-development centers enjoy public funding of more than $2 billion annually.

One mistaken message that these programs advance is that the world is eager to have more entrepreneurs and will welcome them with open arms. In reality, however, the market is seldom happy to see a new company. Many entrepreneurs with great new ideas quickly learn that their innovations threaten markets occupied by big companies. Apple and Microsoft had to survive the efforts of big computer companies, including IBM, to put them out of business. Big companies have reason to fear the challenges startups present; two giant computer companies, Wang and DEC, did not survive the innovative threats that Apple, Intel, Cisco, Dell, and Microsoft posed.

Today, taxi cartels in many cities are attempting to block Uber, Lyft, and other ride-sharing startups from disrupting their hold on local markets. In various cities these companies cannot operate without breaking the law, being fined, and having their drivers arrested and their cars impounded. Competition in business is for keeps.

## Your Life As an Entrepreneur

As you read this, about nine million Americans are thinking about starting a company. On average, they will kick the idea around for at least three years. Only about 500,000 will start new companies this year. Starting a business is an exciting prospect. Yet, as the numbers suggest, many shrink from choosing to become entrepreneurs.

Because the likelihood of failure is so high, everyone searches for a map before starting the journey. Writing a business plan has long held the promise of making your decision seem a bit more rational and the desired outcome, a successful business, somewhat more predictable.

Reality suggests that the value of this type of detailed and rigid planning is minimal. Most entrepreneurs dig right in, start their businesses, and plan as they go along. Success won't yield to a plan. Rather, success is more likely the product of the entrepreneur's motivation, experiences, and readiness to learn and adapt—a path that reveals itself only after he takes the leap of faith in the first place.

The potential return from starting a company that flourishes, however, is measured not just in money and the earned identity of being a successful entrepreneur. While these are the goals that motivate every entrepreneur in the beginning, most find that, if their ideas succeed, if customers buy their new products, they begin to look at things a little differently. They start to understand that what they do helps people live better, safer, and happier lives. They also know the sense of accomplishment that comes from building a successful organization. New companies create jobs for others and wealth for the whole economy. While Bill Gates has become one of the richest people in history, the money he made is a tiny fraction of the expansion of human welfare that Microsoft made possible and continues to produce.

If our most successful entrepreneurs had written business plans, humanity might never have enjoyed the undeniable benefits that their companies have generated. That is reason enough for you to chart a different path to becoming an entrepreneur. If you've already written a business plan, take my advice: Burn it!

# Acknowledgments

Ewing Kauffman died ten years before I learned of his foundation. It was my good fortune to meet him through Anne Morgan's biography and her subsequent service as one of the original trustees of the Kauffman Foundation. I owe enormous gratitude to Anne, John A. Mayer, Ramon de Oliveira, Thomas J. Rhone, and the late Siobhan Nicolau and Brian O'Connell, whose fidelity as trustees to Kauffman's aspirations for his foundation was inspiring. Kauffman researchers and colleagues, Bob Litan and Dane Stangler, helped me form many of the insights that follow.

I have been blessed by great teachers in life who taught me how to connect empirically established facts to actionable conclusions. They include Professors John P. White; W. Lee Hansen; Rogers C. B. Hollingsworth; the late Robert M. Heyssel, MD, president of The Johns Hopkins Hospital; and Michael Novak of the American Enterprise Institute.

I am especially thankful for faculty colleagues and students at Syracuse University with whom I am privileged to work and teach. Elizabeth Liddy, dean of the School of Information Sciences, is an entrepreneurial academic leader of the first order and the best of campus friends. Jake Smarr provided much appreciated research assistance, and Lois Elmore is always two steps ahead of me.

ACKNOWLEDGMENTS

AJ Sidhu managed the manuscript and much more with good cheer throughout, for which I am grateful. Alice Martell, the best of agents, patiently and graciously provided needed encouragement.

Every author thanks his family. In my case, my wife, Ellyn Brown, was an indispensable spur and source of ideas, for which I am deeply grateful.

Finally, I remember my ultimate go-to source for perspective on entrepreneurs, Paul Magelli. An economist on the faculty at the University of Illinois for more than forty years, Paul died as I was completing the manuscript. He was a model of what a great professor should be—insightful, wise, and extravagantly generous to students, each of whom became his friend for life. I am lucky to be in the legion of those whose lives he brightened.

# Notes

### Preface

1. Joseph A. Schumpeter, *Capitalism, Socialism and Democracy*, 2nd Ed. (1942; Floyd, VA: Impact Books, 2014).
2. William E. Baumol, "Entrepreneurship in Economic Theory," *American Economic Review*, May 1968.

### Chapter 1: Burn the Business Plan

1. I found there was no evidence of higher prices in cities where for-profit companies owned more than one hospital. Because of government and insurance payment protocols, it was hard to extract monopoly profit. Carl J. Schramm and Steven C. Renn, "Hospital Mergers, Market Concentration and the Herfindahl-Hirschman Index." *Emory Law Journal* 869, 1984.
2. The commonly accepted elements of business plans are as follows: product description, estimate of market size, analysis of potential competitors, story of founder's decision to start company, description of the startup's team, detailed marketing plan, description of pricing strategy, operating and production plan, analysis of risks, financing required, exit strategy.
3. Basil Peters, *Early Exits: Exit Strategies for Entrepreneurs and Angel Investors (but Maybe Not Venture Capitalists)* (Coquitlam, BC: MeteorBytes, 2009).
4. "Our Credo." Johnson & Johnson, October 3, 2016.

5. Richard L. Florida, *The Rise of the Creative Class: And How It's Transforming Work, Leisure, Community and Everyday Life* (New York: Basic, 2002).

6. Daniel Kahneman and Amos Tversky, "Intuitive Prediction: Biases and Corrective Procedures," *TIMS Studies in Management Science* 12 (1985): 313–327.

7. Albert O. Hirschman, *Development Projects Observed* (Washington, DC: Brookings Institution, 1967).

8. The identity of the entrepreneur is so attractive that it has been expropriated by many people starting organizations historically known as charitable, voluntary, or eleemosynary. Today someone starting a nonprofit is commonly said to be a "social entrepreneur." Most nonprofits, however, do not produce innovations that respond to market needs, where price determines the value of goods or services. The "customers" of nonprofits are philanthropic donors or governments who "buy" services on behalf of beneficiaries. This is one reason nonprofits, certainly those not benefiting from government support, seldom experience scale growth. It is impossible to find nonprofits that have grown like Airbnb, Facebook, Uber, or SnapChat. Carl J. Schramm, "All Entrepreneurship Is Social," *Stanford Social Innovation Review*, June 2011.

9. William J. Baumol, *The Free-Market Innovation Machine: Analyzing the Growth Miracle of Capitalism.* Princeton, NJ: Princeton University Press, 2002.

10. opportunitylives.com/how-wal-mart-serves-the-poorest-americans/.

## Chapter 2: Twelve Things Every Aspiring Entrepreneur Should Know

1. William Baumol, Robert E. Litan, Carl J. Schramm, *Good Capitalism/ Bad Capitalism* (New Haven, CT: Yale, 2009).

2. The oldest formal corporate effort is the Johnson and Johnson Development Corporation. Established in 1975 to create strategic partnerships with startups, it often provides capital to support early research efforts and clinical trials.

3. "Entrepreneurial Impact: The Role of MIT," Kauffman Foundation, 2009.

4. Robert E. Litan, *Trillion Dollar Economists* (Hoboken, NJ: Wiley, 2014).

5. "Inc. 500 Reveals America's Fastest Growing Private Companies," http://www.inc.com/news/articles/200410/inc500.html.

6. Maria Bustillos, "How VCs Turned My Startup into a Nightmare," https://www.buzzfeed.com/mariabustillos/confessions-of-a-dot-com -entrepreneur?utm_term=.x10rPXN.

7. U.S. Census Bureau, Annual Survey of Entrepreneurs, 2014, http:// www.census.gov/programs-surveys/ase.html.

8. "10 Steps to Finding the Right Co-Founder," https://www.entrepre neur.com/article/244259.

9. "18 Mistakes That Kill Startups," http://paulgraham.com/startupmis takes.html. See number 1.

10. "Thinking of Going Solo? 7 Reasons You Need a Co-Founder," https:// www.entrepreneur.com/article/239945.

11. "Breaking a Myth: Data Shows You Don't Actually Need a Co-Founder," https://techcrunch.com/2016/08/26/co-founders-optional/.

12. "Absolutely, DO NOT, get a co-founder!" https://news.ycombinator .com/item?id=77246.

13. "18 Mistakes That Kill Startups," http://paulgraham.com/startupmis takes.html. See number 17.

14. Acton School of Business, http://www.actonmba.org/about/teachers /jeff-sandefer/.

15. In some business schools, half of students majoring in entrepreneur-ship intend to work in nonprofit startups. California is the cradle of nonprofit corporate experiments. See http://www.nonprofitlawblog .com/california-social-purpose-corporation-an-overview/.

## Chapter 3: Why Start a Company?

1. Betsy Morris, "Overcoming Dyslexia," *Fortune*, May 13, 2002.

2. *Journey into Dyslexia*, HBO documentary, directed by Susan Ray-mond, 2011.

3. See https://www.youtube.com/watch?v=9wNgJEuLktE.

4. Joan M. Finucci, Linda S. Gottfredson, and Barton Childs, "Follow-Up Study of Dyslexic Boys." *Annals of Dyslexia* 35 (1985): 117.

5. Derek Thompson, "The Government Is Horrible at Predictions (So Is Everybody Else)," https://theatlantic.com/business/archive/2013/12 /the-government-is-horrible-at-predictions-so-is-everybody-else.

## Chapter 4: What Motivates Entrepreneurs?

1. https://www.quora.com/How-long-do-you-have-to-be-a-street-cop-be fore-going-into-homicide-detective.
2. *Major Discoveries, Creativity, and the Dynamics of Science*, Rema-print Wien, 2011.
3. "The Case for Music in the Schools," *Phi Delta Kappan* 75.6 (1994): 458–459.
4. Christopher Hitchens, *Letters to a Young Contrarian* (New York: Basic, 2005).
5. *The Origins of Modern Science*. Bell, 1950.
6. Sharon Weinberger, *The Imagineers of War* (New York: Knopf, 2017).
7. Included are resort hotels, theme parks, and sport-equipment manufacturers. Twenty percent of all phone apps are for entertainment.
8. In 1950, a twenty-year-old business student named Warren Buffett invested in GEICO, calling it the most undervalued company in the market. In 1995, Buffett's investment company, Berkshire-Hathaway, acquired the entire company.

## Chapter 5: Can You Survive the Entrepreneur's Curse?

1. "New Racquet—It's Smart," *Des Moines Register*, December 26, 1976.
2. Fitzgerald, Eugene, Andreas Wankerl, and Carl J. Schramm, *Inside Real Innovation: How the Right Approach Can Move Ideas from R&D to Market—And Get the Economy Moving* (Singapore: World Scientific, 2011).

## Chapter 6: Big Companies Can Be Schools for Startups

1. *The Protestant Ethic and the Spirit of Capitalism* (Allen and Unwin, 1930).
2. E. M. Schimmel, "The Hazards of Hospitalization," *Annals of Internal Medicine*, 1964, 60-100-110. Also, Lucian L. Leape, "Error in Medicine," *Journal of the American Medical Association*, December 21, 1984, 272, 23, 1851.
3. Albert O. Hirschman, *Exit, Voice, and Loyalty: Responses to Decline in Firms, Organizations, and States* (Cambridge, MA: Harvard University Press, 1970).

## Chapter 8: Preventing Failure Before It Happens

1. Patients with the drug showed a slight treatment effect.
2. Kamen is also the founder of FIRST Robotics, a now global robotics competition designed to encourage high school students to study engineering.
3. Every patent ever granted is now instantly accessible. See http://patft.uspto.gov/netahtml/PTO/search-bool.html.
4. https://www.fastcompany.com/3059230/the-theranos-scandal-is-just-the-beginning.

## Chapter 9: Don't Waste Time Doing Things That Don't Work

1. Richard Feynman, "Cargo Cult Science," 1974, see http://wwwcdf.pd.infn.it/~loreti/science.html.
2. Barton H. Hamilton. "Does Entrepreneurship Pay? An Empirical Analysis of the Returns to Self-Employment," *Journal of Political Economy* 108, No. 3 (2000).
3. In fact, it wasn't true. Jackson was acquitted, but evidence notwithstanding, he was banned from Major League Baseball and endured lasting public approbation.
4. AnnaLee Saxenian, *Regional Advantage: Culture and Competition in Silicon Valley and Route 128* (Cambridge, MA: Harvard University Press, 1994). Saxenian's work echoes Michael Porter's earlier "cluster theory" of national development, which suggests that countries should leverage their competitive advantages in natural resources, labor skills, and technology to foster industrial growth. See Michael Porter, "Location, Competition, and Economic Development: Local Cluster in Global Economy," *Economic Development Quarterly* 14, 14–34.
5. Fewer than seventeen percent of incubators reported data in a recent survey. See Linda Knopp, *State of the Business Incubation Industry*, NBIA Research Series (Athens, OH: National Business Incubation Association, 2012).
6. Alejandro S. Amezcua, "Boon or Boondoggle? Business Incubation as Entrepreneurship Policy," https://www.maxwell.syr.edu/uploadedFiles/news/BoonOrBoondoggle.pdf.
7. As one professor of entrepreneurship has observed, "Most of the incubators that I visit are publicly subsidized real estate operations. Their

primary goal seems to be to full occupancy of buildings. As long as they receive rent from tenants and governments they have achieved their objective. In some sense, if a company grows out of its space they have a problem—they need a new tenant." Private correspondence with author.

8. The Foundry, formed by several firms in 1998, is an early example. Venture firms hoped they could make their own deals by finding and supporting promising entrepreneurs.

9. Brian Solomon, "The Best Startup Accelerators of 2015," https://www .forbes.com/sites/briansolomon/2015/03/17/the-best-startup-accelera tors-of-2015-powering-a-tech-boom/#4672c1d867ca].

10. See http://www.seed-db.com/accelerators.

11. See http://www.leeds.ac.uk/educol/documents/00001500.

12. See http://www.slideshare.net/FranckNouyrigat/mentors-and-mush rooms.

13. Malcolm Gladwell, *The Tipping Point: How Little Things Can Make a Big Difference* (Boston: Little, Brown, and Company, 2000).

14. Thomas S. Kuhn, *The Structure of Scientific Revolutions* (Chicago: University of Chicago Press, 1996).

15. Eric Ries, *The Lean Startup: How Today's Entrepreneurs Use Continuous Innovation to Create Radically Successful Businesses* (New York: Crown Business, 2011).

## Chapter 10: Planning for Success

1. Richard Kihilstrom and Jean-Jacques Laffont, "A General Equilibrium Entrepreneurial Theory of Firm Formation Based on Risk Aversion," *Journal of Political Economy* 87 (1979): 719–748.

2. Hongwei Xu, Martin Ruef. "The Myth of the Risk-Tolerant Entrepreneur," *Strategic Organization*, 2004.

3. https://www.edge.org/conversation/the-adjacent-possible.

4. http://www.pucpr.br/noticia.php?ref=1&id=2014-12-08_54855. See also https://www.theverge.com/2016/10/6/13184094/apple-app-academy -opens-italy.

5. Robert Coram, *Boyd: The Fighter Pilot Who Changed the Art of War* (Boston: Little, Brown, 2002).

6. Pilot-to-pilot confrontation became obsolete with heat-seeking missiles.

## Chapter 11: Becoming a Successful Entrepreneur

1. Francis Arthur Jones, *Thomas Alva Edison: Sixty Years of an Inventor's Life* (T.Y. Crowell, 1908).
2. http://www.1millioncups.com/.
3. https://startupweekend.org/.
4. https://www.blackstonelaunchpad.org/.
5. http://www.techshop.ws/.

# Index